The Happier Approach

ALSO BY NANCY JANE SMITH

Juice Squeezed: Lessons Learned from a Quest to Live Happier

This Stuff Is Hard: Making Peace with Your Anxiety

The Happier Approach

BE KIND TO YOURSELF, FEEL HAPPIER, AND STILL ACCOMPLISH YOUR GOALS

Nancy Jane Smith

Live Happier Publishing
Columbus, Ohio

All Rights Reserved by Nancy Jane Smith LLC
Printed in the United States of America
ISBN: 978-0-9912505-3-0
Library of Congress Control Number: 2017919720

Live Happier Publishing
1550 Old Henderson Road S202
Columbus, Ohio 43220
www.Live-Happier.com

Cover Design and Character illustrations: Amelia Street Studio
Editing: Amy Scott

To my Dad, whose Monger won until the bitter end. Thank you for being my Biggest Fan. I love you.

Rest in Peace
Ted A. Smith
1938–2017

Contents

CHAPTER EIGHT

CHAPTER NINE

CHAPTER TEN

CHAPTER ELEVEN

Introduction

After almost 20 years of working with people as a coach and counselor, I have come to realize that the #1 thing that prevents us from feeling happier is the negative voice in our head. You know the voice, that mean nasty voice, telling you your hair is too gray, you are a terrible mom for not making it to the soccer game, or you failed yet again by not speaking up at work.

That voice. I call that voice the Monger.

Most of us have a Monger. My Monger has always been loud and mean. She had a lot of rules and standards for how I should live my life. My Monger convinced me that happiness and success can't be obtained without hard work and punishing myself. Perfection is the standard my Monger held me to, and she convinced me that happiness and contentment are always one step away.

I graduated from a small Catholic high school in middle America and made my way to a Midwest university doing all the "right" things as explained to me by those around me. I spent much of my 20s muddling my way through, oscillating between the beliefs that *I can do anything if I only know what that is* and that I must *be practical, get a good job in business, get married, buy a house, and settle down.*

During this time, my Monger continued to hammer me and told me that if I pushed myself hard enough and checked off all the boxes (i.e., good job, nice house, supportive husband), *then* I would be happy. She was happy to push and scold me until I achieved the next item on the list, and I was happy to listen.

In my 30s, I had what looked like a successful life: a Master's degree, a job I enjoyed at a local college, an active social life, and a new house. I had checked off (almost) all the boxes. In all honesty, I wanted for nothing and I was supposed to be happy. And still, I remember sitting on my porch with my then good friend now husband saying, "I have a good job, a loving family, and a nice house. I *should* be happy. What is wrong with me?!" He nodded and smiled and poured us more wine.

I look back on that time and cringe—hello, privileged!? And yes, I have been very privileged in my life. But it is easy to get stuck in self-blame and privilege. In truth, I wasn't just whining; I was lost. My Monger was telling me constantly how lost, stupid, and incompetent I was. It didn't matter how much money, success, or privilege I gained; my Monger always wanted more. She kept happiness dangling like a prize I could win if only I was a better person. Unfortunately, no matter how hard I tried, I never seemed to win. I was successful—or at least my Monger had bullied me to a place of what looked like success—but I wasn't happy. I was miserable.

The Monger is universal. She knows no color, economic, or social bounds. She haunts all of us. Telling us how much we miss the mark, how terrible we are, and how much more we should do to succeed. It doesn't matter if we have all the money in the world. We can't buy out our Monger.

Over the next few years, I started seeing a counselor, and eventually I was inspired to earn my Masters in Counseling. I learned a lot about the Monger both personally and professionally, but I never learned how to successfully quiet her. For the most part, my Monger controlled my life, causing me to be more anxious. I call it Hustling for Happiness, this belief that success and happiness are just out of reach. My Monger keeps me hustling with the belief that *this* time I will do it perfectly. Once I achieve X (losing 20 pounds, getting the next promotion, getting married, etc.), *then* I will have arrived. Even as I taught about the Monger and shared with people the dangers of this negative voice, I was secretly getting eaten alive by my own Monger.

Around this same time, my dad's health began worsening and I started spending more time with him. I always knew he lived with a loud Monger, but I had no idea how strong a hold his Monger had on him. In his lifetime, he had loved the same woman for 53 years, built his own insurance agency from scratch, raised three loving kids, given back to the community, and worked to maintain a beautiful home. Now, he was a man in his 70s ravaged by Parkinson's with Dementia. He fought every day to keep moving and stay active. When he looked back on his well-accomplished life, he still didn't feel good enough. His Monger convinced him that no matter what he did, he was a failure. I swore to myself things had to change. I had to start doing my life differently I wasn't going to spend my time on earth being hammered by my Monger.

So I started on a quest. I read as much as I could about how to quiet the inner critic (aka Monger). The advice was to love yourself no matter what (aka practice self-compassion), so I became obsessed with the subject of self-compassion. I chatted with clients and friends. I practiced self-compassion exercises like repeating positive mantras and telling myself how awesome I was.

To be honest, the idea of loving myself no matter what was radical and foreign. It sounded great, but it wasn't something I could do 100 percent of the time. Hell, I couldn't even do it 20 percent of the time. I couldn't do it because secretly I equated all the success I had achieved so far with how hard I drove myself. In other words, I believed my Monger when she repeatedly told me that success equals happiness and success only comes when you are hard on yourself.

This idea of self-compassion left me questioning: If I loved myself no matter what, could I still be successful? What about being happier? Could I still accomplish as much? Or would my to-do list just grow and grow while I sat eating Reese's cups and bingeing on *The Real Housewives*?

It was an internal struggle. I didn't want to turn into my dad, never feeling enough and always looking for the next thing, but I also didn't want to be an aimless loser who never accomplished anything.

The problem was twofold: One, my Monger voice was painful and stressing me out. Two, when I practiced what I thought was self-compassion, it would lead to a short respite, but in the end, it made my Monger *more* fired up. I realized that just finding self-compassion was not enough.

I was living in this constant back and forth between the extremes of my Monger and the false "do whatever you want" version of self-compassion. Ultimately, my Monger always won. She always convinced me that I wouldn't accomplish anything without her constant correction.

I believed that I needed my Monger to accomplish my goals. I saw this belief in my clients too. Whenever I would speak about the Monger, I would always get pushback. They believed they needed their Monger to be successful. They believed that without their Monger criticizing them, they wouldn't get out of bed to work out, stop at one drink, speak up at the meeting, or rush across town to make it to their kid's soccer game.

Why are we listening to something that is causing us pain? Because growing up we learned that at our core we are useless human beings and without the constant direction of our Monger we would be lumps on the couch, bingeing on Netflix and doughnuts while our home and lives lay in ruins. But the problem runs deeper. It isn't the voice itself; the problem is our belief that we need the voice to accomplish our goals in life.

Because we believe that we need the voice of the mean, shaming Monger, the idea of giving ourselves compassion and kindness is completely foreign. Our Monger convinces us that the one thing we need the most—kindness and compassion—is the thing that will keep us unsuccessful and unhappy.

The good news is that after years of researching, studying, and trial and error I figured out a process that worked not only for me but the hundreds of clients I have worked with individually and in groups. It is a way of looking at our Monger and at self-compassion differently. I now have control over my Monger rather than letting her run the show.

I teach this strategy to my clients and it is incredible to watch clients go from feeling stressed out and beaten down to feeling confident and in control. Yes, they still get stressed, and yes, their Monger still takes the mic, but her voice is no longer the only game in town. The constant berating and always feeling one step behind success is gone. We now have a way of working around her that allows us to move on with our lives and the goals we want to accomplish.

This book explores that process. We will look at our Monger, at false self-compassion masquerading as our BFF, and my favorite character, the Biggest Fan.

My hope is that through reading this book you will learn that you don't have to live overwhelmed and stressed out. You don't have to beat yourself up to become a "better" version of yourself. And you don't have to be a full-time meditator to do it. Through implementing the strategies in this book, you can be kind to yourself and feel happier—and still achieve your goals.

This book is designed to help you unhook the belief that to accomplish anything you need to be constantly beating yourself up. It is for those of you who realize that living with this constant attack isn't helpful and yet secretly feel like you need it to not be a complete lump on the couch all the time. If you have a love-hate relationship with your Monger, this is for you.

CHAPTER ONE

Meet Your Monger

According to the *Merriam-Webster.com Dictionary*, a monger is "a person who attempts to stir up or spread something that is usually petty or discreditable."[1]

That voice in our head is trying to stir shit up. Our Monger tells us how much we suck, that we are total failures, terrible parents, worthless employees, and all-around losers. (Sound a little harsh? Listen to yourself one of these days and I bet you'll see that I'm not too far off.)

Your Monger was put into place when you were a child. Throughout your childhood, you learned the right and wrong ways to behave, the behaviors that were valued, and the goals you were expected to achieve. Sometimes those messages were sent by an abusive parent smacking you across the face for lying. Sometimes they were sent by a teacher correcting you for crossing against the light. Quite honestly, the how doesn't really matter. *How* your Monger got there is not as important as *what* her behavior is and how her behavior affects you now.

In my work, I have found that our Mongers all have individualized themes, usually inspired by messages we heard growing up. While my Monger may have a heavy focus on being perfect, someone else's Monger may have a heavy focus on people pleasing and making sure everyone around them is happy. Bottom line, your Monger is a voice in your head whose message makes you miserable.

In addition to making us miserable, our Monger causes our anxiety to increase, leaves us exhausted and frustrated, and can keep us stuck and immobilized.

The truth is, the Monger's job is to keep us safe. Her sole mission is to scan the environment for any potential harm, risk, or danger and protect us from it. Her mission is to keep us safe from failing. I have found she has three main rules to help her complete this mission:

1. Don't make a mistake.
2. Don't stand out.
3. Don't be too vulnerable.

If any of those rules are broken, she uses shame, belittling, guilt, and negativity to move us back in line.

When we try something new or take a risk (no matter how small), our Monger gets scared for us and wants to keep us safe. Unfortunately, your Monger has a perfect memory. She catalogs and recalls every failure, mistake, or doubt you ever had and isn't afraid to use them against you on this mission to keep you safe. In an attempt to protect you from making a mistake, she will remind you of every failure you've ever made.

If we attack our Monger using her methods, it rarely works. If we tell our Monger to shut up, she will just fight back harder. More importantly, this voice is a part of us. Telling a part of us to "shut up" or "quit being a bitch" just doesn't work. Fighting shame with shame never works.

Just like the evil witch who locked Rapunzel in the castle to keep her innocence safe, your Monger convinces you that she is there to protect you. That you *need* her to keep you from looking stupid or failing. But really this is all just a bunch of propaganda. Lies, pure lies!

You don't need to be shamed and belittled to be successful. This is the part that no one believes so I will say it again: you don't need to be shamed and belittled to be successful. I spent *way* too many years of my life believing that the Monger was my friend, that she really supported me and wouldn't lead me astray. But after years of listening to her and constantly feeling bad about myself, I decided there must be a better way.

Let me introduce you to Samantha. Notice how the Monger uses shame and belittling to "motivate" her.

> *Beep, beep, beep!* Samantha's alarm breaks the morning silence. Bleary eyed and half awake, she reaches for her phone to shut off the alarm. Just five more minutes, she thinks. As she taps snooze and burrows under the covers for five more minutes of bliss, that familiar Monger voice starts chatting. "Come on, Samantha, you said you were going to work out today! Those pounds aren't just going to melt away. You are so lazy."
>
> I know, she thinks, but I just need five more minutes. I will just shower extra quick, and the kids can take the bus to school. I *need* five more minutes.
>
> "Yeah, yeah, yeah," her Monger growls, "we all know how this goes. 'Five more minutes' turns into five more, and before you know it the time you allotted for working out has been slept away. You are always going to be fat, out of shape, and lazy."
>
> Samantha drags herself out of bed and grabs her running shoes. Grouchy, tired, and resentful, she heads out for a run.

Yes, Samantha's Monger motivated her to get out of bed and work out. Her Monger's message sounds good: To prevent failure (the ultimate goal) you must do your best (nothing less than perfection), don't stand out, and don't be too vulnerable.

But in reality, Samantha paid a heavy price for that motivation: resentment, stress, feeling like a loser, and exhaustion. Her Monger motivated her, but at what cost?

Conclusion

Because your Monger believes she is there to keep you safe, protected and successful, she acts like she is your friend. But in reality she is making you miserable. She is constantly preying on your insecurities in order to keep you small and part of the status quo. She drives you to be perfect when perfection doesn't actually exist (even though she is *really* good at convincing you it does).

You want to feel successful, fulfilled, and happier, yet you have this voice in your head chiming in all day long about how you missed the mark. You will *never* feel successful as long as you are listening to the Monger. She will always make you feel insecure. Your search for feeling "enough"—powerful enough, strong enough, happy enough, successful enough—will never be fulfilled as long as you are listening to her.

Knowing that the Monger isn't necessary is the hardest part of this work. The Monger is *so* good at convincing us that we need her. When I work with clients, this is where they repeatedly get stuck.

For now, start noticing how often your Monger chats at you and how often you believe her message.

CHAPTER TWO

Myths That Keep Us Stressed

When you think about your life, it is probably full of stress: a to-do list a mile long, work demands, home demands, relationship demands. We are dealing with raising our kids and helping our aging parents all while building a career and trying to keep our relationships hot and spicy! It is *a lot.*

Our day-to-day life is stressful. And if you throw in politics and the state of our world, it is no wonder that we are a nation full of anxiety.

Recently I stumbled upon this quote by Julie Peterman and thought, Yes, this sums it up perfectly:

> "Our capitalist culture celebrates productivity so much that we overwork ourselves to the point of extreme depression, anxiety, crumbling relationships, and deep self-hatred and still measure ourselves successful." [1]

The truth is our plates are too full, but rather than being kind and encouraging to ourselves, we listen to our Monger criticizing us, telling us how we haven't quite measured up, we aren't happy, thin, grateful, or successful enough.

From what you choose to eat to how you talk to your kids, your Monger will always have a running commentary about you and your behaviors. All day long, she chats at us telling us where we have failed to hit the mark. And even if you accomplished everything on your to-do list, made your family a home-cooked meal, and ended the day by having hot sex with your spouse, your Monger would *still* come up with something you failed to do.

But here's the thing. For many of us, we are so used to the Monger talking that we don't even hear her anymore. We just take whatever she tells us at face value. We assume that the negative voice, the "you will never measure up" message is the T-R-U-T-H. This is one of the reasons the Monger is so hard to quiet. Literally, there is a voice in our head that is beating us up because we will never be perfect, leaving us feeling exhausted and overwhelmed. We hate how the Monger makes us feel but don't even notice that the Monger is chatting non-stop. It's like wearing high-heeled shoes, and all day long your feet hurt. You complain about the blisters and how much your feet hurt but never recognize that it's your shoes causing the pain.

We can break free. The first step is starting to notice when the Monger is talking. From an early age, we were sold a series of myths that our Monger convinces us are the truth. We fall under the trance that if we live our lives according to these myths (or truths, according to the Monger), we will be happy and successful. But it is an impossible goal, a metaphorical straitjacket. Learning to recognize these myths is one way to build awareness that your Monger is running the show.

Our Monger lives in absolutes. She looks at the world in black and white, right and wrong, so she tries to convince us of absolute truths that are basically completely false. I call these untruths the Myths of the Monger.

These myths have three things in common:

1.   They are designed to protect us from failure. They keep us trapped in chasing perfection, following the status quo, and not being vulnerable.

2. They are unattainable. We will *never* reach the finish line that these myths are selling. So the victory that we are sold will happen never actually does. These myths will never make us happier or more fulfilled.

3. They force us to constantly look outside of ourselves for the secret to happiness. These myths keep us from trusting ourselves. And the only way to be happier and more fulfilled is to stop looking outside of yourself for the answers.

As we start noticing these myths playing out in our lives, we can build awareness of our Monger and her message that keeps us trapped. We can shine a light on our Monger's absolutes and start to loosen their grip.

THE MYTH OF THE FINISH LINE

From a young age, we were told there are life goals that we should want, and once we have achieved all those life goals, *then* we will be happy. Our Monger, always wanting us to be safe and not stand out, convinces us that once we hit these so called "finish lines," then we can relax and be safe. So we set out to accomplish these goals on the search for the finish line of happiness.

The problem is that with each new goal we accomplish, we are quickly met with a new goal.

- Graduate college: Where are you going to work?
- Get a promotion: When are you going to settle down?
- Get married: When are you going to have kids?
- Your kids head off to college: You ask, Is this all there is? Wasn't I supposed to feel more fulfilled than this?

Throughout this book, I'll be sharing stories from the life of Samantha. We met Samantha earlier as she was struggling with waking up early so she could work out. Samantha is a go-getter, high-achieving woman who struggles regularly with her Monger. She's a composite based on real women I've worked with, kind type-A women who are trying to balance caregiving for those around them with finding personal fulfillment and success.

Here's a bit more background on Samantha:

In her 20s, Samantha spent most of her time moving up the career ladder and looking to find a life partner. By the time she was 30, Samantha had been made a manager at her firm and was making good money, she and her partner had just gotten engaged, and she was busy planning a wedding. By age 35, Samantha was a senior manager, married with two kids, and well on her way. At age 45, Samantha was VP and had two kids aged 11 and 13, a house in the suburbs, and a partner who loved and supported her.

Behind the scenes:

In her 20s, Samantha was constantly obsessing about finding a life partner. She didn't want to be old and single; she wanted to share her life with someone. Samantha worked long hours and went on countless dates. It was exhausting but she knew once she earned the manager title and found a life partner then life would be better. By age 30, Samantha had made manager, but if she was honest, she was bored of her job and questioning whether it was the right fit for her. But she was making such good money she couldn't really leave, and she was getting married soon, so she poured all her energy into planning her wedding and honeymoon. Once you get married and have your family, *then* you will be happier, she told herself.

Through her 30s, Samantha moved up in her job, again working long hours, but she was mostly focused on having and raising her family. Juggling everything was exhausting, and she and her husband started to move down separate paths. There was just so much to do, it was hard to keep everything organized and prioritized. She kept telling herself, You are doing it. This is life. Keep plugging along. Once you get the kids off to school, *then* you will have more time to enjoy life.

By 45, Samantha continually found herself waking up in the middle of the night asking herself, This is it, right? I mean I did everything right; why am I so unhappy? It just didn't seem to be getting any easier. She and her husband loved each other but had grown apart. Her job was okay but not at all as fulfilling as she had hoped. She loved her kids and always felt guilty that she was a terrible mom.

Samantha's finish line was constantly moving, her Monger convincing her happiness was just around the corner. And yet at the end of the day, she was left feeling tired, exhausted, and never enough. Finally, she asked herself, Is this normal? When she looked around at her friends and family, they all seemed to be running on the same treadmill to nowhere.

It's ironic: our Monger convinces us that once we accomplish the next goal *then* we can relax, celebrate, and feel accomplished. But the finish line keeps moving. The finish line keeps moving because it is an external marker. A continually moving prize that we are chasing because we think getting there will bring us peace, joy, happiness, success, or calm. But that feeling of peace, joy, happiness, success, and calm does not come from our accomplishments.

The Myth of the Finish Line perpetuates a never-ending cycle. We don't feel happy, so we set a goal that we think will help us feel happy. We set the goal based on what people tell us we *should* want, but when we accomplish the goal, we still don't feel happy. So we set about accomplishing another goal; we tell ourselves this time *this* goal will be the key to feeling happy, rinse and repeat. All the while our Monger keeps telling us the myth that everyone else is happy, not struggling, and enjoying their lives at the finish line.

Alanis Morissette's song "Incomplete" perfectly describes the unsatisfying chase of the Myth of the Finish Line. Here's my favorite part of the song:

> *"I have been running so sweaty my whole life*
> *Urgent for a finish line*
> *And I have been missing the rapture this whole time*
> *Of being forever incomplete"*[2]

Beat the Myth Tip

The first step is beginning to question this myth. Notice how often you convince yourself, When I accomplish _____, then everything will be okay. Start asking yourself, Do I want to accomplish ____? Or is that a message from somewhere else (e.g., childhood, society, friends, family, etc.)?

Spend some time looking at your day-to-day activities and seeing how often you push yourself in the quest for a finish line. Lovingly remind yourself that you are "forever incomplete." There is no finish line.

SOME STRAIGHT TALK

The Myth of the Finish Line is one of the most challenging of all the Monger myths because it permeates everything we do. We are constantly asked about, praised, and judged by our accomplishments. It is not only an internal message from our Monger but an external message from society.

As a society, we believe that accomplishments will make us happier. For me, I found that learning how to break free of that praise and judgment takes time. The first step is recognizing how empty, stressed, and overwhelmed the constant quest for accomplishment makes us. The quest keeps us hooked: if we are judged we work harder to get it right, and if we are praised we work harder to earn more praise. It is never enough.

THE MYTH OF THE GOOD PERSON

Our Monger is always trying to keep us safe from failure by encouraging us to be perfect, not to stand out, and not to be too vulnerable. The Myth of the Good Person encompasses all three of those. The Monger tells us that *if* we are a "good" person without flaw, *then* we will only receive compliments and never deserve criticism.

We make up all kinds of rules about what it looks like to be a good person. For example, a good person

- never calls in sick,
- always makes a home-cooked meal,
- works out five days a week,
- always puts others first,
- doesn't need help,
- controls her feelings,
- is always confident,

- is always kind to everyone,
- never says no, and
- is always willing to go out.

The problem with these rules is that like the myth of the finish line the definition of a good person is constantly changing. You never really "win." Even if you are a size 6, you change the rule: a good person is a size 6 *and* can run five miles. Or a good person maintains a size 6 for three years in a row. Or even more impossible, a good person is a size 6 without struggling.

The good person rules are a double-edged sword. On one hand, they make us feel safe and comfortable because we are trying to be a good person. But in reality, they keep us walking on a never-ending treadmill doing "what a good person does" while our reward dangles there in front of us, always out of reach and constantly changing.

In her book *Radical Acceptance,* Tara Brach tells a story that really struck me and perfectly illustrates this idea. It's about a woman whose mother was dying. On her deathbed, the mother opened her eyes and said, "You know, all my life I thought something was wrong with me, what a waste."[3]

When we buy into the story that we are not good enough just as we are and must hustle for worthiness, we are on a losing mission.

When we believe this myth, our Monger forces us to live in a black-and-white world where there is only *good* and *bad*. This is the world of the Monger, and there is no other color in this world. The real world is full of color. But when we are buying into this myth, we speak in absolutes: "never" and "always" become a regular part of our language. In the real world, there is room for "sometimes" and "occasionally," as well as mistakes, risks, and apologies.

Beat the Myth Tip

Pay attention to your good person rules. As you start noticing them, write them down or say them out loud. The goal is to start noticing the voice of the Monger and separating her voice from your own. Notice how often you use the words "always" and "never." When you notice the black-and-white thinking, ask yourself if there are other options. Is there a way to see the other colors rather than just living in black-and-white?

THE COMPARISON MYTH: *THEY* HAVE IT FIGURED OUT

You know *those people*: our friends, family, and acquaintances we interact with and see on social media. *They* look like they have it all figured out. To learn about what we *should* be doing or how we *should* be behaving, we go out into the world and gather information. We try to find out what are *they* doing so then we will know how to behave in the world. We do this through conversations, observations, and—the most toxic— social media.

It's a typical Saturday. You sign on to Facebook and see that your acquaintance Liz has decided to take a spur-of-the-moment day trip to go hiking and canoeing and has posted a picture of herself, sun-kissed and smiling, holding a beer as she sits next to the river. She says something cutesy about being blessed. As you sit in your pajamas surrounded by piles of laundry, you immediately feel insecure and your Monger starts chatting, "You never take these spur-of-the-moment trips. Hell, you don't even take *planned* trips that look this fun. You *should* be more hip and flexible."

with looking at the magical *they* is that you are
ur insides to someone else's outsides. And as we
never goes well.

ror all you know, Liz's husband had to drag her
to go hiking and canoeing. Or maybe Liz and her
husband fought the whole drive to the river. You
saw one photo that captured a moment in time.
Maybe Liz took 10 photos before she found that
perfect shot. And here you are beating yourself into
a bloody pulp over it.

That is the danger of social media. It is so carefully curated
that we only see the final product. We only see what *they* want
us to see, which may not be the reality. A study by researchers
at the University of Houston[4] found a relationship between the
amount of time spent on Facebook and depressive symptoms.
In other words, a tendency to engage in social comparisons on
Facebook can cause us to be more depressed.

Our Monger loves to point out what *they* are doing as a way
to help us not stand out. Our Monger wants us to fit in, and the
best way to fit in is to see what *those* people are doing and
shame us when we aren't doing it just like them.

One of my favorite quotes about the power of our uniqueness and the danger of comparison comes from dancer Martha
Graham:

"There is a vitality, a life force, an energy, a quickening
that is translated through you into action, and because
there is only one of you in all of time, this expression is
unique. And if you block it, it will never exist through
any other medium and it will be lost. The world will not
have it. It is not your business to determine how good it
is nor how valuable nor how it compares with other ex-

pressions. It is your business to keep it yours clearly and directly, to keep the channel open."[5]

Beat the Myth Tip

Notice when you start comparing your life to other people's lives and remind yourself that the Monger is not in charge here. Lovingly remind yourself that *they* don't have it figured out any more than you do.

Frequently we see other people doing activities and we think we should be doing that activity too. If you find yourself doing this, stop and ask yourself, Is this an activity I want in my life? If yes, explore how you can add more of that activity to your life. If no, wish *them* well and move on. Remember, we all act like we have it figured out, when in reality no one's life is perfect. We are all doing the best we can with what we have, imperfectly.

THE MYTH THAT THERE IS A RIGHT WAY

The Myth that there is a Right Way is a little harder to spot. This myth is like all the others because it has just enough juice to keep us hooked. Not surprisingly, people who are looking for the right way tend to be perfectionists. We rationally know there is not one way to do anything; there is no "right way." Yet we spend our lives looking for it: the right way to drive, eat, work out, cook, do a project, trim a tree. You name it, we can look for the right way. This myth leads us to a life of black-and-white thinking where there is an absolute *right* way and an absolute *wrong* way in all situations. Our Monger believes finding the right way will protect us from being attacked or criticized externally.

Here is a simple example from my own life to show how sneaky these myths can be.

One day I was in the kitchen making a peanut butter and jelly sandwich. As I gathered the bread and the peanut butter, I realized I was trying to make the perfect sandwich. To me, the perfect sandwich meant I was able to make it with the most efficiency. The least number of steps or trips around the kitchen. I was simply making a PB&J lunch for myself. Nothing fancy. I was not trying to impress anyone. And yet my Monger was telling me there was a *right* way. I laughed to myself and asked myself, What would I win if I did it right? And more importantly, how would I know I did it right? Who were this imaginary judge and jury that were judging me?

When you start to pull apart these "right way" myths, you start to see the faulty logic. Doing it right is subjective. Who decides "right"? When it comes to "doing it right," the ironic thing is that right is subjective. Let's go back to that perfect PB&J sandwich. For one person that might mean the right blend of peanut butter and jelly; for another person that might be making it as beautiful as possible. For me it was making it as efficient as possible, and for someone else maybe right means always using grape jelly and chunky peanut butter. Maybe the perfect sandwich is on white bread or maybe wheat bread. Right is subjective. We will always fall short of doing it right.

As all good perfectionists know, there is no winning. Even if we make the perfect sandwich by our standards, we will always find something wrong with it. As I said, efficiency is a "right way" measure for me. When I go to the grocery store, I have a lot of rules on how to do it right. But even if I accomplish my task in the most efficient way possible, I still beat myself up for *something*. I never celebrate the win. Maybe I didn't pack the groceries in the car right or I forgot to pick up soap or I picked the wrong checkout lane. I always fail.

When we buy into this myth, we get stuck in all-or-nothing thinking. One way to notice this myth playing out in your life is when you make if-then statements:

- If I don't go to the grocery store on the way home then I am a bad mom.
- If I don't work late then I will get fired.
- If I commit to a dinner date then I will be stuck the whole night.
- If I don't work out today then I will be out of shape forever.

See how those statements are absolutes of right and wrong? Your Monger will never give you the win—you could always have done it better. But in all honesty, there is no *right*. There are no absolutes. It is a myth that keeps us chasing our tails and pulling our hair out for something that has no real meaning.

Beat the Myth Tip

When you catch yourself engaging in all-or-nothing if-then statements, challenge yourself to come up with as many options as possible. Even if they seem absurd, get in the practice of expanding the options.

For example:

If I don't go to the grocery store tonight,
Then I can go tomorrow after work,
or I can ask my partner to go, *or* I can bring a cooler to work and grab a few things on my lunch hour and do the big shopping on Saturday.

If I don't work out today,
Then I can look at my schedule and find the best time to fit in a consistent workout. Maybe it would be best to do it in the morning, or at lunch, or turn

some of my regular work meetings into walking meetings.

THE MYTH OF WORRY AND VIGILANCE
(AKA SPINNING OUR WHEELS)

Our Monger convinces us that worrying is helping. If we worry about something, we are *doing* something to prevent attacks and pain. But the truth is, worry just begets worry. Worrying, rehashing, and spinning our wheels do nothing to help the situation. We convince ourselves we are being vigilant, but unless we are solving a problem in a very real way we are just worrying to be worrying.

> Think of a warm cozy sweater that you find in the back of your closet. It has been worn in and fits just right. Worry is like that sweater. You slide into it and think, Ah, yes, now I am safe. This is comfortable and familiar. Then slowly over time you realize why this sweater was buried at the back of your closet: it's itchy! Soon that comfortable familiar feeling gets taken over with itching, scratching, and wanting to get the sweater off as quickly as possible. Our Monger convinces us that worry is that sweater and every time as we start to worry, we think, Yes, this is so comfortable, safe, and familiar. Then over time we realize, Oh no, I just feel worse, this is not comfortable at all. And yet our persistent Monger convinces us to pick up the worry again, over and over and over.

We become addicted to worrying. What if everyone laughs at me? What if no one shows up? What if she thinks I am a bitch? What if I get sick? and on and on. We overplan and overthink almost everything to control the situation and make it less scary. Isn't that ironic? We are trying to make the situation less scary, but in reality we are thinking up as many terrible things that can happen as possible!

Here is the painful truth. Life is out of our control. They might laugh at you, no one might show up, they might think you are a bitch. Thinking and planning is not going to prevent that. Worrying is not going to make your insecurities suddenly go away or make you feel more worthy.

I remember years ago sitting on my therapist's couch discussing this very problem and she said, "All you are doing is Mental Masturbation." The crude reference made me gasp at first. But the more I thought about it, the more accurate it was. I have tried to find another term but have never found one that describes the condition so well. Because the Catch-22 is, we know it isn't helpful, but it initially *feels so good*. And that fact is what makes it so hard to unhook it. Not impossible, just hard. It is a breakable habit.

The truth is the more we worry and spin out on a certain topic, the more it spotlights the fear and insecurity we have about that topic. This means we need to be kind to ourselves around that topic, not hammer ourselves with more worry and fear.

Beat the Myth Tip

Worrying is such an automatic response for us that we have a hard time noticing when we are engaging in it. It helps to notice the behaviors you engage in when you are worried (e.g., obsessive list making, overeating, picking at your nails, playing with your hair, excessive exercising, etc.). Catching yourself engaging in the behavior is easier than noticing the thoughts around worrying.

When you notice the behaviors, lovingly remind yourself that worrying isn't productive. Our Monger keeps us stuck in the perpetual loop of "what if..." To counter that, be honest about your fears and concerns and take each of them out to the worst-case scenario. Usually it isn't as bad as your Monger leads you to believe, and recognizing that allows you to develop actual strategies rather than just the constant loop of worry.

THE MYTH THAT WE NEED THE MONGER

Finally, the ultimate myth: the Myth That We Need the Monger. We believe that without the Monger telling us how much we suck and what we need to do next, we will not accomplish anything. It wasn't until I started challenging this myth that things started shifting for me.

I touched on this myth in the Introduction and Chapter 1, but it bears repeating because this is the ultimate myth that is keeping you stuck in Mongerville.

Our Monger wants us to be safe and fit in, so she pushes us to be perfect and not stand out. Her method of motivation is to be critical, beat us up, and shame us. In our attempt to avoid the criticism, we try harder to be perfect, to not stand out, and to not be vulnerable. From the outside, it looks like we have a lot of motivation because every time the Monger is critical, we push harder. Because of this pattern we convince ourselves we need the Monger in order to achieve success.

It is easy to see how we can believe this myth. The fear of the Monger's criticism has been an amazing motivator. And it has worked—we have accomplished life goals and achievements—but it has also left us feeling beaten up and bruised.

Slowly, over time, we start to see that this myth isn't true. We start to see that all this criticism and shame is just making us feel more stressed and exhausted. The Monger has benefited us, but at what cost?

Here is how this myth shows up in Samantha's life.

Samantha has been asked to do a presentation at work. Because of her fear of giving the presentation and a lack of time, Samantha has procrastinated until the night before to do her PowerPoint presentation.

As she sits in front of her computer, she hears her Monger chime in, "How could you be so stupid to wait until the last minute. You are always procrastinating and look where it got you, working late and cramming in these slides. You aren't going to do your best work because it is so last minute. You are such a loser. You should have been working on this weeks ago."

Samantha grabs a sip of coffee and slumps over in her seat. Ugh, she is right. I totally should have worked on this before. My procrastination is such a problem. I am going to be up half the night because I waited so long.

Is the Monger helping? Yes, Samantha did procrastinate, and yes, she does have to finish the presentation, but the Monger throwing that up in her face isn't really helping. It is just making her more stressed out and exhausted.

We wouldn't do this to a child, would we? Take Joey, who enters second grade unable to read. Truth be told, there are lots of reasons and people to blame, but the bottom line is Joey can't read. Joey's teacher doesn't say to him, "You are so stupid, how did you make it to second grade without learning how to read? Wow, your parents really failed you." No, Joey's teachers meet Joey where he is. Because he can't read and they can admit that, they don't waste time beating him up about that fact. They simply help him read. They help him get to the root of the problem (e.g., his fear or lack of desire or knowledge) in order to move past whatever is in his way.

If Joey's teachers were critical of his inability to read, he might be motivated to learn simply to avoid their criticism, but he would dread school and not be excited about learning new things. But if they meet him where he is, accept that he can't read, and skip the part where they beat him up about it, he can learn a lot faster and develop a love of learning.

Similarly, if Samantha met herself where she is with kindness and said to her Monger, "You know what, you are right. I did procrastinate on this project for a variety of reasons *and* I will get it done. I don't need you chiming in all night telling me how awful I am, so quiet down."

Admitting that we don't need the Monger's shame is an important step in moving past it. Because the truth is we can't change anything until we own it. Our Monger keeps us stuck in blame and criticism. She never allows us to move past the shame so we can see what we need to do to move forward.

The bottom line is we don't need the Monger. We are going to accomplish more by accepting ourselves where we are and working with what we have rather than constantly berating ourselves. I promise, you will accomplish more without listening to your Monger. You will be happier, more successful, and sleep better.

Beat the Myth Tip

When you notice the Monger blaming and criticizing you in an attempt to motivate you, try to remove the blame and criticism. Try to separate fact (what you need to own about the situation) from fiction (the shame and criticism).

Think of yourself as an eight-year-old child. What would you say to that eight-year-old who needed some motivation? Would you criticize her or would you kindly offer solutions?

Here are some examples.

- Want to get back in shape? Own what areas you must work on to get back in shape.

- Want to get over your fear of speaking? Own what you are most afraid of when it comes to speaking.

Simply beating yourself up for being out of shape or for your fear of speaking won't help anything. You must face the problem so you can then work on it.

CONCLUSION

These myths have one thing in common: they keep our minds busy on thoughts that don't serve us. The myths keep us chasing our tails. After years of following the rules, being a "good person", and not making any waves, we are left feeling disenfranchised and disappointed.

Yet the Monger still chatters on telling us how much further we have to go. We drive ourselves so hard and talk to ourselves so cruelly. We know it doesn't feel good. We know it isn't working anymore, but learning how to change the pattern, and believing that you can accomplish stuff without beating yourself up, is hard. It took me *years*. I want to shorten the process for you so you can free yourself from these myths and quiet your Monger much faster than I did.

CHAPTER THREE

What Doesn't Work and Why

There are a lot of tips out there on how to be happier and more successful. Most of them talk about how to think positive, be more grateful, and be kind to yourself.

"Let go of those negative thoughts."
"Be kind to yourself."
"Give yourself what you need."
"Accept your worth."

When I first started my therapy practice, I taught the concepts of repeating mantras, being grateful, and changing your thoughts because that was the common wisdom.

To be honest, I was practicing them in my own life and they weren't working, but everyone told me they should work, so I was secretly hoping that somehow through teaching these concepts their magical healing powers would do something for me. But they didn't. In fact, I became stuck in a cycle of beating myself up even more because I was teaching something I *knew* wasn't working.

At the time, I didn't know a better way. Today, I have found a better way, and my clients feel a sense of relief when I tell them they don't have to repeat a bunch mantras or simply "think positive."

Western society has taken the concepts of self-compassion, gratitude, and positive thinking too far. Whenever a concept gets turned into an all-or-nothing way of being in the world, it is trouble. Let's take a deeper look.

SELF-COMPASSION RUN AMOK

Researchers asked 5,000 people to rate themselves between 1 and 10 on 10 habits identified from the latest scientific research as being key to happiness.[1] All 10 habits were found to be strongly linked to life satisfaction, with acceptance as the habit that predicts happiness most strongly.

Yet acceptance was also revealed as the habit that people tend to practice the least, generating the lowest average score from the 5,000 respondents. When answering the question about acceptance— "How often are you kind to yourself and think you're fine as you are?"—people's average rating was just 5.56 out of 10. Almost half of the respondents go through life feeling not good enough and beating themselves up for it.

I believe we practice acceptance the least because we don't know how. Our whole lives we have been told to keep plowing forward, to achieve, achieve, achieve, and no matter how much we succeed it is never quite good enough.

I remember in my early 30s, when I was desperately trying to find some peace and happiness in my life, I stumbled upon a self-compassion concept where you ask yourself repeatedly throughout the day, Do I accept myself as I am, right now? I remember thinking, I *love* that question. It is a powerful question. Yes! I *love* this idea. I am going to ask myself this question. But every time I asked myself the question, I would end up debating: How can I accept myself and achieve my goals? Doesn't the idea of accepting myself no matter what mean I don't need to grow anymore?

It didn't take me long to realize that truly being able to answer that question would require more personal growth; at the time, I had no idea what it meant to accept myself just as I am. My whole life, the idea that I was not worthy just as I was had been reinforced. I needed to be more successful, smarter, thinner, married, single, pregnant, or something other than what I was at that moment.

Eventually, I grew discouraged with the concept of acceptance/self-compassion. How was I going to do the #1 thing to make me happier (love myself) when I believed it made me a failure? I believed if I tried to accept myself as I was, I would settle for a life of being lazy and unaccomplished. I wanted to be successful, and I had a lot of goals left to accomplish. I didn't see how compassion was going to get me there. I had been taught and fully believed the only path to success was through my Monger—if I didn't beat myself up all the time, I would not be successful. I was caught between settling and success.

I know I am not alone in this thought process. I often give presentations on stress reduction and the Monger, and when I talk about self-compassion and how important it is to be kind to ourselves, I see multiple heads nodding in agreement. I will even get the occasional "yes" or "amen" from the audience. Inevitably, when there is a break and everyone heads out to the hall for snacks, I hear women talking about how they shouldn't have a cookie, beating themselves up for breaking their diet or being a fat ass. And I wonder, what happened to all those head nods?!?

There are so many quotes and motivational sayings that sound lovely but are challenging to put into practice. I did a quick google search for "love yourself quotes" and came up with 9,960,000 results, such as:

"Love yourself for what you are instead of hating yourself for what you are not."

"When you undervalue what you do, the world will undervalue who you are."

"Love yourself first and everything will fall into line."

"No one is going to love you if you don't love yourself."

"Don't forget to love yourself."

Raise your hand if your social media feed is full of these quotes. Raise your other hand if the walls of your office or the pages of your journal are full of these quotes. They sound nice, but studies have shown that repeating these quotes doesn't help. In fact, psychologists at the University of Waterloo concluded that such statements make people with low self-esteem feel worse.[2] Repeating positive mantras may benefit people who already feel good about themselves but backfire for the very people who "need" them the most. For those people, trying to feel "good enough" by repeating mantras doesn't help.

Apparently, Stuart Smalley had it wrong. Telling yourself, "I'm good enough, I'm smart enough, and doggone it, people like me" won't make you feel better about yourself. There are so many people telling us the positives of self-compassion. We *know* it is necessary for our lives. But it is like someone handing us a brand-new IKEA chair with no instructions. We might really want the chair, but we can't figure out how to put it together.

I have found this over and over when it comes to the idea of self-compassion. It is a profound idea that we all love in theory. Yet it can be confusing and troublesome to put into practice on a daily basis. Especially for those of us who have this secret love for our Monger and believe we *need* to have that voice telling us what to do next, even if her message leaves us feeling exhausted and stressed.

If the myth that we need the Monger is running the show, then sometimes we practice what I call false self-compassion. This is when we do whatever we want under the guise of self-compassion. False self-compassion looks like we are being kind to ourselves, but in reality we are just acting like a rebelling child and doing the complete opposite of what our mean Monger tells us to do.

When we have had enough bullying, and berating from our Monger, we rebel by doing whatever we want and justify it by saying we are practicing self-compassion. This looks like overeating, overdrinking, procrastinating, or any other way in which we go against our own good in the name of self-compassion.

We love the *idea* of self-compassion, and it is in fact the answer to reducing the voice of our Monger. Yet repeating mantras, reading quotes, and practicing false self-compassion will not get us closer to accepting ourselves in a lasting way. The following tips, however, will.

Tips for Self-Compassion

Remind yourself you can be kind to yourself *and* achieve your next goal. Think of yourself as an eight-year-old who wants to ride a bike. To encourage the eight-year-old, you would start by doing an assessment of their strengths and weaknesses and then moving forward from there. You wouldn't judge or shame them for their weaknesses; you would just notice them.

Notice when you are practicing false self-compassion. Self-compassion does not mean permission to do whatever you want. When you catch yourself rebelling against your Monger, ask yourself, Does this really serve me, or will I "pay a price" later? If you will pay a price later, it isn't self-compassion.

Pause. When you read a mantra or like a quote on Facebook, take a moment to pause and breathe it in. Really think about the quote. What does it mean to "love yourself for what you are instead of hating yourself for what you are not?" Throughout the day, pause and think about the quote or idea and notice where you struggle with it.

THE BASTARDIZATION OF "THINK POSITIVE"

Thinking positive is the belief that if we simply change our thoughts, we can change our lives. Thinking positive and seeing the bright side has its helpful qualities. But when we use thinking positive as a tool to hammer ourselves, it becomes less helpful.

I see this all the time in my office, where clients will stop themselves mid-vent to say:

"I should be happy but…"
"I don't mean to complain but…"
"I have a great life but…"
"These are champagne problems but…"
"I know I am so blessed but…"

Here's how "think positive" affects Samantha's life as she takes care of her mom.

As she walks up to the front door of her mom's house, Samantha is greeted by her mom, half-dressed and looking frazzled and exhausted. "Did you pick up my prescription?" she asks in a panicked voice. "I *have* to have my pills!"

"It's okay, Mom," Samantha sighs as she pulls out the bag of pills "I have it. Everything is okay."

On top of her mom duties to her 11- and 13-year-olds, Samantha is also primary caregiver for her mom, who was recently diagnosed with Alzheimer's. Her dad died a year ago, and although her brothers are helpful, they don't live locally and can only do so much. After a frenzied visit, Samantha climbs back in the car, late for her son's cross-country meet.

Samantha's Monger chimes in: "Way to go, Samantha, you just keep dropping the ball, don't you?

You promised Matt you wouldn't be late. You know you need to find a home for your mom. She is not safe in that house by herself. And work—your boss already said you can't miss any more days this month. You are going to lose your job on top of everything else."

Samantha takes a deep breath. She read recently that when she gets negative, she should try to think positive. "I have a wonderful marriage. Mom is going to be fine. I get to spend all this bonus time with her. And everything will work out just fine." As she starts naming the positives, tears sting her eyes and start streaming down her face. She is just so tired and discouraged.

"Suck it up, butter cup," her Monger laughs. "You think you have it so bad. At least you can afford to send your mom to an assisted living community. You know there are people out there who aren't as lucky as you. It could be so much worse. And here you sit. Crying your eyes out. You are such a whiner. At least your mom is still here. You can't even do it well and you have the support of a caring husband and family. I mean imagine if you were divorced and trying to do all of this."

Ouch. Talk about positive thinking gone wrong. But sadly, that tends to be the way of our Monger: positive thinking can become ammunition for shaming and belittling.

Positive thinking can also put us into denial and leave us without a plan of attack. If Samantha keeps looking on the positive side, she will never be able to care for her mom the way she wants to. Not only will she be exhausted but she won't have a good plan.

Gabriele Oettingen, a professor of psychology at NYU, has done several studies on the dangers of positive thinking and how it impedes our ability to face long-term problems (such as caregiving).[3] Through her research, she has discovered that thinking positive can prevent us from seeing the situation clearly and being able to develop realistic solutions. When we engage in positive thinking, sometimes we don't allow ourselves to feel the complexity of the situation.

Let's go back to Samantha:

> Tears stream down Samantha's face. Quietly she says to herself, This is so hard *and* it is understandable you are so tired. Take a breath and look around at the trees. Mom loved trees; remember how she would take you out and you would lay on your back looking up at the trees. Such a rush of feelings thinking back to those times. You are so grateful for them and yet they make you so sad. That's okay. Both are true. You want Mom to live the rest of her life feeling safe and happy. We need to all sit down and have a plan to figure out how we are going to continue to care for her long term.

As Oliver Burkeman, author of *The Antidote: Happiness for People Who Can't Stand Positive Thinking*, says: "A positive thinker can never relax, lest an awareness of sadness or failure creep in. And telling yourself that everything must work out is poor preparation for those times when they don't."[4]

When we are afraid of the "negative" side of life, we become hyper-vigilant and more stressed. Looking at our lives honestly instead and owning that everything isn't awesome allows us to make a realistic plan for the future.

Tips for Thinking Positive

Be honest with yourself. It all starts with honesty. Honestly admitting your mistakes, challenges and weaknesses without blame and criticism. When you can be honest without the judgment then you can begin to make real change.

Beware of black-and-white thinking. Too much of anything is too much, so too much negativity can be just as bad as too much positivity. Challenge yourself to see all sides of the situation, not just all the positive or all the negative.

THE DOWNSIDE OF GRATITUDE

In a similar vein to think positive is the concept of gratitude. Don't get me wrong, I am a *huge* fan of gratitude when practiced correctly. I believe we have taken gratitude to an extreme (as we tend to do in this culture). We take gratitude so far that it becomes a weapon our Monger uses to criticize us.

Gratitude is an amazing practice. It allows us to be thankful for the little things in our life and to see the world through a different lens that is more positive and clear.

When used correctly, gratitude allows us to:
- Recognize and appreciate the little things in our lives.
- Change perspective and concentrate on what matters.
- Get unstuck.

Gratitude is not meant to be:
- A magic wand that takes away all our pain.
- Fake it until we make it.
- A cover-up for all that is wrong with our life.
- A way to shame ourselves into happiness.
- Something that keeps us stuck in a place of punishing ourselves for feeling anything negative or remotely ungrateful for anything in our lives.

I call this the downside of gratitude. When we name what we are grateful for as a way to discount or diminish our real problems and pain, it is a definite downside.

When I talk about the downside of gratitude, I frequently get pushback, and I am used to people coming up to challenge me on the concept. So when a woman approached me after one of my presentations, I was prepared for her to push back, but instead, she grabbed my hands and looked me in the eyes and said,

> "Thank you. I have breast cancer and I haven't really processed it or felt anything about it because I kept telling myself I should be grateful that it isn't worse, when in reality it has been really hard. Yes, I am thankful it isn't worse, and what I have been dealing with is hard!"

When gratitude prevents us from seeing our lives for what they truly are, when it causes us to mask and hide the pain in our lives, it isn't serving us.

Too often, I hear people saying:

> "They have it worse."
> "At least I am not..."
> "Be grateful I don't have..."
> "I should be feeling grateful..."

This approach to gratitude is not just painful; it is stifling. We ignore the reality of the pain in our lives because we tell ourselves we *should* be grateful, when instead we can feel the pain *and* be grateful. Like the woman who had breast cancer: she can be grateful for the fact that it was a curable form of breast cancer *and* be sad and scared that she had to experience cancer. Ignoring the pain she experienced and painting it prettier with gratitude doesn't take it away.

Whenever Samantha has doubts or insecurities about her life her go-to behavior is practicing gratitude.

Samantha loves her husband and their relationship. She wishes they communicated better and were more intimate, but she stops those thoughts frequently by telling herself she has it better than most and she should be grateful. He treats her well and isn't cheating on her, and although they don't talk about much other than work and the kids, she loves him and enjoys their life.

Samantha's job is extremely stressful. Her Monger is always chatting at her telling her how behind she is. Her boss is a terror and enjoys managing through shame and belittling. Samantha tries so hard to juggle all the expectations he has for her and all the expectations she has for herself at home and in her life. She knows they need the money from her income, and she is so specialized it would be hard to find something different at this point. She tells herself she should be grateful. A lot of people don't have the opportunities she does.

Samantha is so tired of feeling not enough. She is tired of her schedule dictating her life. She is tired of her friends saying, "You have a great life, you have it all together, how do you do it?!?" But inside, Samantha feels like a failure. She just wants to be happy, or at least happier. She is tired of pretending, and she just doesn't know how to slow down this crazy treadmill she is on. How did she get here, to this place where she always wanted to be, and yet it just isn't enough? What is wrong with her? How can she be so ungrateful for her life?

Samantha can't win. She's stuck in the same vice in which many of my clients are stuck. On one hand, she has what appears to be a great life. She has all the trappings of success. She has all the things we are all told to go after, achieve, and gain in our lives, and she is happy with those things. From the outside, her life looks incredible. Samantha is grateful for that, *and* on the inside, it is a very different story. Samantha is overwhelmed by her Monger constantly telling her where and how she has failed. She wants more from her life but she doesn't quite know what that means. And the minute she starts noticing she wants to make some changes, or that her life isn't what she wants it to be, she hammers herself with thoughts of being ungrateful and unworthy.

She stops herself from exploring her thoughts, feelings, and needs by telling herself things like:

"It could be worse..."

"You have it so good..."

"This is what you wanted for your life..."

"You should be celebrating."

Samantha has even spun the phrase "be grateful" into a belittling, hurtful phrase.

Here's the thing:

Truth: Samantha has a great life and is grateful.

Truth: Samantha wants more out of her life.

Both are true and that is okay.

Samantha has a great life, beautiful kids, a loving marriage, and a beautiful home, *and* Samantha wants more. Not more *stuff,* not more *success,* and not more of what people told her she *should* want.

Samantha wants more *depth,* more *intention,* more of *what's real* for Samantha.

It's a new paradigm: Samantha can be grateful *and* want something different for her life. Once Samantha accepts that both ideas are true, then she can make positive changes.

Too often, our Monger takes gratitude and uses it to keep us stuck in shame and guilt. Instead, lovingly remind yourself you are grateful that you do have a great life *and* that doesn't mean you should settle. You can be dissatisfied *and* grateful *and* want more.

Tips for Gratitude

Go deep not wide. Get as specific as possible, such as "I am so grateful for my daughter's hugs in the morning." When we are generic with our gratitude, it tends to boomerang back to self-criticism.

Practice the *and*. *And* allows us to hold two opposite truths. I feel sad *and* I am grateful for the sunshine lighting up my office right now. I wish my mom wasn't sick *and* I am glad my husband is willing to listen to me vent.

Recognize it is okay to feel bad. Shit happens. Life is hard. No one said we were supposed to be 100 percent happy all the time. Give yourself a break!

CONCLUSION

Self-compassion, positive thinking, and being grateful are helpful concepts, but when they are practiced in a way that prevents us from being honest about our lives and accepting our pain and challenges, they keep us stuck. It is harder to grow and achieve if we are constantly pushing our weaknesses down by telling ourselves to just "think positive" or answering our doubts with "be grateful."

Unhooking the traditional ideas of these three concepts is challenging. Because our Monger loves absolutes, it is easy to get stuck in thinking that we should always be positive or always be grateful. When you catch yourself going to extremes with these concepts, pause and remind yourself it is okay to feel. We are supposed to feel a wide range of emotions. Slowly bring yourself back to seeing the bigger picture.

CHAPTER FOUR

The Cast of Characters

We all have voices that chime in our head all day long. They're reminding us to pick up the dry cleaning, telling us how we have failed as a mother, encouraging us to go out with friends, or suggesting that we squeeze in a workout.

The critical inner voice, the Monger, is one most of us are familiar with and the one I have covered at length so far. For years, I have taught about the Monger. Every book I read about the inner critic encouraged getting to know and understand your Monger, so I helped people dive deep into what their Monger was saying, how it was saying it, and what it looked like. But it wasn't helping me or my clients. We knew our Monger's themes and had a visual image for her, but she was as loud as ever.

I started exploring self-acceptance, self-compassion, and the idea that you are supposed to talk to yourself like you are your own best friend. I spent a long time getting to know my inner best friend (I call her my BFF). She was kind and nice, but I quickly discovered she was more of an enabler. She was the opposite of my Monger, encouraging freedom and kindness to counteract my Monger's shame and belittling. Unfortunately, I also quickly noticed that all my BFF did was fight with my Monger. Yes, she had my back. Yes, she wanted me to be happy.

But she wasn't really helping the situation or looking out for my best interests. She was just stirring up drama with my Monger.

I noticed the same issues with my clients. The more we explored self-compassion, the more confused they became. We uncovered the practice of false self-compassion, where we equated loving ourselves with a free pass to do whatever we wanted. Our BFF would encourage cake and chardonnay, only to be met with the Monger suggesting we were fat alcoholics who didn't deserve such treats.

I realized I needed a counter to my Monger, and so did my clients. Something that was like a BFF but that held our feet to the fire like our Monger. A voice that wanted what was best for us and was still able to motivate us in a kind, loving way. A voice above the drama. Enter the Biggest Fan.

It wasn't until I found my Biggest Fan that everything changed for me. Recognizing and naming these three characters was a game changer. It helped me move beyond the myths and the traps of self-compassion and gratitude into a system that worked. It helped me discover how to add self-compassion into my life and counter my Monger.

Teaching these concepts to my clients has been amazing. Learning about and identifying these three characters provides a concrete way of discussing and working with self-compassion in conjunction with our drive to accomplish things in life.

Let's get to know this cast of characters a little more intimately.

YOUR MONGER

You've already met and learned a lot about your Monger. As a reminder, your Monger has two main traits:

1. Her job is to keep you safe from failure. She motivates you by telling you, "Don't make mistakes, don't stand out, and don't be too vulnerable."

2. All her messages bring shame and drama and are exhausting. Basically, she is just outright mean and nasty.

Let's check in with Samantha and her Monger in action:

With tears in her eyes, Samantha walks out of the conference room and makes it to the bathroom just before the waterworks begin. My boss just screamed at me in that meeting. I can't believe I missed that deadline, she thinks. How did I miss it? I spent all week working on the spreadsheets. I didn't realize he wanted me to be writing the copy.

Then she hears her old friend the Monger, "You are going to get fired for this mistake. Did you see how angry your boss was? You totally missed the boat on this one. How could you be so irresponsible? Funny that you stayed late to work on the spreadsheets and that wasn't what was important. Yet again you have your priorities mixed up. You *always* make this mistake; ever since you were a kid you have been a ditz. I just don't get how you can be *that* stupid. You had better stay late tonight and make up for this mistake."

Tears stream down Samantha's face. Her Monger is right. She is a ditz and this time she is going to get fired, she just knows it. She cleans her face up and heads to her desk defeated and stressed. She starts to work on the copy, but all the while her Monger is chatting at her about how much she dropped the ball. By the time Samantha leaves work, she is stressed, exhausted, and feeling like the biggest loser on the planet.

Our Monger is the worst! She adds on to whatever anxiety or fear we are already experiencing. Life is stressful enough without the constant chatter of how we failed yet again.

Your BFF

Our BFF enables us to rebel against the mean voice of our Monger. When we get tired of our Monger criticizing us, we bring in our BFF for a little self-compassion, but it often ends up going overboard into false self-compassion (aka doing whatever you want). Our BFF *loves* false self-compassion.

Your BFF is the one who always has your back, is always willing to risk getting into trouble, is always there to defend you—*that* BFF. She is not about holding your feet to the fire or keeping you accountable, but is always able to find a justification and someone to blame. She is all about helping you feel special. She is kind and wants you to feel good about yourself. In her mind, responsibility, accountability, and restraint do not apply. Listening to her can feel awesome, and she can be trouble.

To our BFF, self-compassion means:

- You are always right.
- They are always wrong.
- You *deserve* whatever your heart desires.
- Fun is #1.
- She will protect you to the death.

Let's check in with Samantha, who is headed to happy hour.

> "Let's get out of here! Thank God it's Friday. I need a drink!" says Megan, standing in the doorway to Samantha's office. Samantha grabs her coat and they make a run for the door. It has been a terrible week and Samantha can't wait to grab a drink.
>
> After her second drink, Samantha tells herself she needs to stop; tomorrow she has an early morning. She promised herself she would work out every other day, and so far she hasn't missed for two weeks straight.
>
> "Have another one!" says Megan, "Your husband is watching the kids and we Ubered here so it will be fine!"
>
> "No, I'm good, I want to get up and work out tomorrow before the kids' soccer games."
>
> "Whaat!?!" Megan says, "are you kidding me?! Tomorrow is Saturday. *Come on*! Don't be a party

pooper. You know you want another one, and we can grab some mozzarella sticks to help soak up the alcohol. Come on, just one more."

"Why not?!" Samantha's BFF chimes in. "I mean it has been a terrible week. You deserve it. You're trying to not drive yourself so hard and practice self-compassion, so you are going to give yourself a break and have fun tonight! It has been a *long* time since you have just cut loose."

"Okay," Samantha laughs and joins Megan at the bar.

The next morning, Samantha rolls over and sees her clock: 7:30 am. She jolts out of bed and then quickly grabs her head as it starts pounding in her skull. Ugh. Not only did she not make it to work out, but she is hungover. She had a great time last night, but now she feels like crap.

"Way to go!" her Monger says. "You are such a lush. You can't say no, can you. You have no self-control and now you are miserable and fat. You are never going to get in shape. Wow! You can't do anything right. You can't keep your word and you are a miserable alcoholic. Hope it was worth it! Now you must sit through an entire day of soccer games with a pounding headache. Nice work."

"Of course it was worth it! A shot of coffee, two breath mints, and you are golden," laughs her BFF.

"Ha! Maybe when you were in your 20s. It is not that easy at 40, my friend. Today is going to suck and you deserve it for being so stupid last night," her Monger is quick to remind her.

See how that worked? In the spirit of "practicing self-compassion," Samantha's BFF steered her in the wrong direction. Was it fun? Yes! Was it the smartest decision considering she had a full day with her family the next day? Probably not.

Let's go back to the earlier story of Samantha missing the deadline at work, and see how her BFF might step in during this situation.

> With tears in her eyes, Samantha walks out of the conference room and makes it to the bathroom just before the waterworks begin. My boss just screamed at me in that meeting. I can't believe I missed that deadline, she thinks. How did I miss it? I spent all week working on the spreadsheets. I didn't realize he wanted me to be writing the copy.
>
> First, she hears her old friend the Monger, "You are going to get fired for this mistake. Did you see how angry your boss was?"
>
> It doesn't take long before her BFF has her back. "Come on, girlfriend, your boss is such an A-Hole. I mean to publicly call you out like that is just rude. You had like five projects last week; how were you supposed to know that the copy was most important. They say communication is the key— where was the communication?!"
>
> Her Monger is quick with a rebuttal, "You are the employee. It is your job to know when stuff is due. You should have asked, but you are such a wimp you were too afraid to ask."
>
> "Ha! Too afraid to ask. That is rich," says her BFF, "you deserve to have some respect. You work your butt off around here and for what? No one even tells you what is due when. It is so disrespectful. You are practicing compassion here so you need to be kind to yourself and give yourself a break. He should have been clearer. He saw that

you were working on the spreadsheet. Why didn't he say something?"

"Come on. Bottom line, you messed up. You are going to lose your job. It's as simple as that," declares her Monger.

And around and around they go.

This war between the BFF and the Monger plays out because we live in an all-or-nothing world. We try so hard to do it right, and we are wound so tight in the goal of following *all* the rules perfectly, that we go from one extreme (Monger = complete rule following) to another (BFF = doing whatever you want).

Because she is the opposite of your Monger, your BFF tends to perpetuate the problem. She just gives your Monger more ammunition.

I won't disagree that listening to your BFF is *fun* and easy. She always knows how to have a good time and she is a welcome relief from the voice of your Monger. For years I was stuck here, going back and forth between my BFF and my Monger. I told myself I was channeling self-compassion and being kind to myself, but in reality, I was just making the problem bigger and more confusing. Their constant arguing and battle of wills left me on a hamster wheel of worry and anxiety.

I also see this with my clients. They get stuck in this pattern of "soldiering on" and listening to their Monger and then releasing the pressure with their BFF's false self-compassion.

Finding that middle ground is hard, but it is where the magic is. Because sometimes you need to take responsibility. Sometimes it isn't all about fun and deserving. Sometimes it is about getting stuff done. If we want to fully embrace our lives and do hard things, we have to get stuff done even when it is uncomfortable. And that is where our Biggest Fan comes in.

SOME STRAIGHT TALK

A lot of people love their BFF, and letting go of her partying, fun, rebel ways seems impossible. That's okay. Find a way to incorporate some of that rebellion into your everyday life so that it isn't causing you or those around you more anxiety. Our BFF is so much fun and we don't want to lose that, but when she runs amok and causes us to turn our backs on our goals and dreams, then she can get us in trouble. You don't have to let go of your BFF cold turkey. Slowly start building awareness of her and notice how often she sabotages you rather than contributing to your end game.

YOUR BIGGEST FAN

Now we come to my favorite character. Your Biggest Fan is the key to quieting your Monger. She is the one who will help you achieve your goals and be happier. Your Biggest Fan is the *how*. She is kind, generous, and wise and always has your back. She's the best of both worlds. She holds the goals of your Monger (to be safe and secure) without the shaming and belittling, and she provides the support of your BFF ("you are awesome") without the free pass to do whatever you want.

Your Biggest Fan is the voice that says,

> "You are having fun. Slow down and take a breath. Do you really need another drink? You have been kicking butt on your workouts this week. You want to get up and work out tomorrow *and* you feel so much better when you work out. You can stay and have fun without drinking more, so you won't be hungover tomorrow."

> "Yikes, that is totally scary that your boss called you in tomorrow. Take a breath and do a quick stretch. It will all be okay; no matter what happens we will figure it out. Let's do some brainstorming. How can we best prepare for that meeting?"

Your Biggest Fan has this wonderful combo of kind, wise, and honest (sometimes brutally so).

The #1 thing I hear from clients when I discuss the Biggest Fan is, "I don't think I have one of those." Let me be the first to say that you do have a Biggest Fan. Trust me. Even when you don't think you do, you do. You have that voice inside of you that wants you to succeed.

Your Biggest Fan is probably quiet right now, which is why you might think you don't have one. She has been ignored for so long that her voice is meek, but over time, as you listen to her more and more, she will become louder and louder.

The acronym A.S.K. represents the strategy I use and teach my clients to use to quiet the Monger and bring in the Biggest Fan. When you hear your Monger chatting away or you notice your BFF and Monger fighting, stop and A.S.K. your Biggest Fan for support.

Here are the three steps of A.S.K.:

1. **Acknowledge what you are feeling:** When the Monger tries to shame and belittle you, the Biggest Fan acknowledges what you are feeling (e.g., you must be tired, scared, angry, sad, etc.). She labels your feelings and normalizes whatever your experience is.

2. **Slow down and get into your body:** When the Monger tries to speed you up and make everything more intense, your Biggest Fan allows you to slow everything down, encouraging you to take a break, pause, and breathe.

3. **Kindly pull back to see the big picture:** When the Monger just sees doom and gloom and engages in black-and-white thinking, the Biggest Fan sees lots of colors. She encourages you to think of different solutions, brainstorm, and see the other colors. We tend to be harsh on ourselves when we are looking for new solutions. As we shift from black-and-white to color, the Monger might step in more. That's why doing it kindly is the key.

We will be exploring each of these steps in more detail in later chapters.

Let's return to the story of Samantha missing the deadline at work, and see how she can A.S.K. her Biggest Fan to step in during this situation.

With tears in her eyes, Samantha walks out of the conference room and makes it to the bathroom just before the waterworks begin. My boss just screamed at me in that meeting. I can't believe I missed that deadline, she thinks.

Then she hears her old friend the Monger, "You are going to get fired for this mistake. Did you see how angry your boss was?"

It doesn't take long before her BFF has her back. "Come on, girlfriend, your boss is such an A-Hole. I mean to publicly call you out like that is just rude."

Samantha says to herself, I need to hear from my Biggest Fan. She starts with:

A. (Acknowledge what you are feeling) *Sweet Pea, stop torturing yourself! This is so hard. Doing it wrong sucks, especially when you thought you were doing it right! I get it that you are scared you might lose your job. That is understandable after getting yelled at. It is just embarrassing and humiliating to be yelled at in a staff meeting.*

S. (Slow down and get into your body) *Let's take some deep breaths. It's okay to cry; getting yelled at in public is the worst. Let it out and then we can figure out what comes next.*

K. (Kindly pull back to see the big picture) *This is totally avoidable. Next time, let's double-check (even triple-check) with him on what is his top priority. I know it is annoying (and let's admit it, sometimes scary) to double-check, but it's better than this feeling right now. Your co-workers get it. They have been called out before too. And truthfully, getting fired is probably a bit extreme. Go talk to your boss, clear the air, and figure out next steps.*

See how her Biggest Fan helps Samantha find the middle ground? Her Biggest Fan is kind and understanding but also wants her to do her best and succeed. She isn't enabling. She isn't belittling. She is just there, a kind, wise, motivating voice.

She is the best of both worlds, self-compassion *and* motivation. She is 100 percent kind *and* wants you to be the best version of you. Maybe even a version you can't see yet.

CONCLUSION

This cast of characters has helped me and my clients gain control over the constant chatter in our heads. By implementing A.S.K. I have seen people dramatically reduce their stress and be able to concentrate on what truly matters to them (instead of what the Monger tells them is important).

You will find your Monger and BFF are by far the loudest of the three voices (your Monger being the *loudest*). I believe they are so loud because we listen to them the most. Because they are so black and white in their message, they make listening to them easier. The Biggest Fan takes a little cultivation, a little more time and diligence. I developed A.S.K. as an easy way to remember how to reach her. In the following chapters, we will be exploring A.S.K. in more detail.

Initially, as you get more familiar with these characters in your own head, it is helpful to simply start labeling them when you hear them. Notice when the Monger or the BFF is chatting. Notice what behaviors draw them out or trigger them to start chatting the most. In the following chapter, we are going to look at common behaviors that we engage in when our Monger and/or BFF are chatting.

SOME STRAIGHT TALK

One thing I hate about self-help books is how they make everything sound so simple and easy, as if you can just A.S.K. and everything will magically be okay. This is a loving reminder that this is a process. It is probably brand new to you, so it will take time and energy.

Being able to hear your Monger and implement the A.S.K. process all the way through is the ideal, but don't expect it to happen all the time. Some days you will be lucky to just get past A. Acknowledge what you are feeling. That is a win! Some days you might make it to S. and be able to slow down and get into your body. That is also a win! This isn't a 1-2-3 system. This is a new way of thinking, a new way of looking at your life. As with anything new, it will take time. Be kind. Go easy on yourself and celebrate the wins.

CHAPTER FIVE

Knowing When Your Monger Is Running the Show

If only it was just a matter of noticing our Monger and then poof she was gone, there would be no need for this book and we would all be living in perfect bliss. The fact is, our Monger tends to talk *a lot* without us noticing her. She plays there in our heads all day long, and she becomes so normalized/comfortable/familiar that we don't really notice her. By the time we notice our Monger, she has already wormed her way into our psyche and we feel completely defeated and hopeless.

The best way to start noticing your Monger is through your behaviors and feelings. Too often, our Monger drives us to act or feel a certain way before we even notice her chatting. This chapter is designed to give you examples of the behaviors you engage in when your Monger is attacking you so you can build awareness of your Monger before she paralyzes you in defeat.

When you engage in one of the following behaviors, simply ask yourself, What is my Monger chiming on about now? Then A.S.K. to hear from your Biggest Fan.

SOME STRAIGHT TALK

As my clients start building awareness of their Monger, the tendency is to punish themselves for being so hard on themselves or not noticing the Monger fast enough. It may sound crazy, but as we begin this work almost every client goes through the step of punishing themselves for listening to their Monger (e.g., "stop slamming yourself so much," "you should be happy, dammit!" or "what is wrong with you!?").

The truth is, you will be shocked how often your Monger chats at you (even if you already think your Monger chats a lot, trust me, she chats even more than you think). So be kind to yourself. This is all about fact finding, not judging. You are simply on a fact-finding mission to see how often your Monger takes the mic. That is it. Not beating yourself up, not judging what it is saying, just noticing.

There is no finish line here. Your Monger will always be the first responder; she will always come to the party. The goal in doing these exercises is to decrease her frequency and her power. I have been doing this work for years and she still shows up. But now I have the tools to deal with her so her influence is much less powerful and debilitating.

Following are some examples of the behaviors that show us when the Monger is running the show and the different ways the Monger, BFF, and Biggest Fan chime in.

Sometimes you will notice these behaviors right away and sometimes you won't notice them for days. Either way is okay.

The key is noticing them and then challenging yourself to A.S.K. to hear from your Biggest Fan.

NUMBING AND OVERINDULGING

Numbing and overindulging can take a variety of forms: eating, drinking, shopping, exercising, playing video games, scrolling through social media, or watching TV. I believe one of the primary reasons we overindulge is because we are trying to block the voice of our Monger. Any activity you do to excess can be a form of numbing to help you avoid the constant chatter in your head.

Often when our Monger chimes away all day, we don't notice it until we have already crossed into the numbing behavior. Our numbing behavior serves as a red flag that our Monger is running the show.

Here's how Samantha reacted to a big day at work:

> Samantha arrives home 30 minutes before the kids. It has *been a day* and she immediately heads to the cupboard to see what there is to snack on. Grabbing a bag of chips and some dip, she heads for the computer. As she munches she flips through Pinterest and lands on a site that has some adorable outfits on sale. Samantha decides a couple new outfits would be awesome for the upcoming family reunion. Before she knows it, she has spent $300 on new clothes that she didn't really need and eaten a whole bag of chips. She hears the kids coming in the back door and she slams her computer shut thinking, Why did I just do that?
>
> Samantha pauses to think back on her day, and she realizes her Monger and BFF have been arguing all day because she had some ideas to help solve the

client's problem so she spoke up more than usual during the staff meeting.

Samantha's Monger growls, "Karen was so mad at you today. She didn't talk to you after the staff meeting. You must have talked too much during the meeting. I mean you had some good ideas, but you didn't have to share them *all*. You totally came across as a bossy know-it-all. You might be doing well at work but is that worth it to lose friends and be seen as a bitch? *And* way to go eating a whole bag of chips and spending $300 on clothes. I thought you told your husband you were done shopping online?!"

Her BFF quickly had her back. "If Karen was mad, that's her problem. It's not your fault she is so afraid to speak up. I mean she needs to grow a pair! You kicked butt in that meeting today. You deserve a little potato chip celebration!! You will need those new clothes because I bet they even give you a promotion and a raise! You will be able to do all the online shopping you want with that new paycheck. Who cares if Karen is jealous. You are on your way to a corner office, girlfriend!"

"Raise?! Oh whatever, you are so delusional to think you are going to get a raise. They won't give you a raise just for being loud and obnoxious. You actually have to *do* something and contribute," says her Monger.

In that moment, when Samantha hears the argument happening in her head, she says, "Okay, where's my Biggest Fan?" and starts to A.S.K.:

A. (*Acknowledge* what you are feeling) First off, nicely done, speaking up in a meeting is not your favorite and I am sure it was scary and hard (plus a little empowering). You can be proud of yourself and insecure at the same time.

S. (Slow down and get into your body) Take a deep breath and just touch your toes. There is nothing wrong with sharing your ideas.

K. (Kindly pull back to see the big picture) I am sure Karen isn't mad at you, but you can always check in with her and see what is going on if you want to know. This speaking up thing is new for you, so of course it is going to be scary! Give yourself a break! The potato chips were delicious. Next time we can make sure we enjoy them rather than eating the bag in one shame-filled bite. And the clothes? Let's see how they look when they arrive. Maybe we can send a couple things back. We need to be conscious of our spending, so whatever we don't send back we need to account for someplace else. "

The Biggest Fan labels what Samantha is feeling and allows her to feel insecure and proud at the same time. Her Biggest Fan encourages her to get into her body and gives her options for how to deal with her co-worker and how to handle her numbing behaviors in the future. She doesn't shame Samantha or belittle her; she looks out for her in a loving, kind way.

Notice your favorite numbing behaviors. When you catch yourself engaging in one of them, like scrolling through social media, ask yourself, What is really going on here? Then start with A. and Acknowledge what you are feeling, and you will hear from your Biggest Fan.

HAVING A 10 REACTION TO A 2 SITUATION

Our Monger chatting at us all day long can cause some tension. That constant undertone of shame and belittling can get annoying. When you have an extreme response to a minor situation, it usually means your Monger has taken over.

Here's an example of a 10 Reaction to a 2 Situation:

> As you are checking your work email, you open a meeting request from your boss. You have no idea what he wants.
>
> Immediately your Monger starts chatting, "This can't be good, you are totally going to get fired. I mean what could he want?! Even if you aren't fired, it can't be good."
>
> "No worries, honey, you are awesome! He loves you. Quit dwelling on the negative and think of how much you have helped him recently. Plus, you saw him flirting with Francine. You can totally threaten him if he tries to fire you," says your BFF.
>
> "Oh, please. You are going to blackmail your boss!? That is a brilliant idea, brilliantly stupid. All I know is you need this job; without it you will be screwed," chimes in your Monger.
>
> Your BFF and Monger debate the whole commute home. When you walk in the kitchen, you see the sink is full of dishes. You immediately start yelling at your kids for not doing the dishes, even though they had no idea they were supposed to do them.
>
> Yes, the dishes are annoying, but they aren't really what you are upset about. The fact that your Monger is torturing you with ideas of getting fired is most likely the stressor that needs to be addressed first.
>
> You say to yourself, I need to hear from my Biggest Fan. Stop and A.S.K.:

A. (Acknowledge what you are feeling) Okay. I get it—
you are scared and anxious about going into your
boss's office. That's understandable.

S. (Slow down and get into your body) Let's do a quick
neck stretch so we can get into our body and slow
down.

K. (Kindly pull back to see the big picture) Let's think
of three things he might want to talk to you about
that have nothing to do with mistakes or getting
fired. Maybe he wants to offer you a promotion,
give you a new job assignment, or tell you that he is
leaving the company. There are countless possible
reasons, and you won't know until tomorrow. So
let's just try to relax and enjoy this evening. You
aren't going to make it any better yelling at the kids,
and we all know that listening to the Monger isn't
going to help.

Your Biggest Fan labeled the feelings you are experiencing:
scared and anxious. She encouraged you to get into your body,
and she helped you brainstorm some reasons your boss might
want to see you. Each of these steps was done with curiosity
and kindness, not judgment and blame like the Monger uses.

Overreacting is normal, and it is common for our Monger to
step in to criticize us for overreacting. Remember, when you
overreact it probably means you are tired of being hammered
by your Monger and you need to deal with what is really going
on. You need to A.S.K.

DRAMA, DRAMA, DRAMA

Sitting around with my girlfriends talking about other people
used to be my norm. It was an unconscious way of making myself feel better and quieting my Monger for a while. If I was

judging people I knew for throwing a bad party, it took some of the pressure off my own insecurities around my social skills. Frequently when you find yourself talking about other people it is in response to something they trigger in you. We see it all the time in the *Real Housewives* shows and *Sex and the City* (I have spent many a weekend binge-watching both). Women gather with their girlfriends to chat about other people, and it inevitably stirs up drama.

After a night of gossiping with her neighbors about Susan's latest party, Samantha feels guilty. As she pulls in the garage she asks herself, Why was I slamming Susan? She is so kind and doesn't deserve that.

Yep, answering this requires a real "come to Jesus" moment. Samantha has to get honest. Here's a hint: The answer probably isn't because Susan is annoying. Or because she threw an expensive party last week. The answer could be that she fires up Samantha's Monger. Susan, who is a stay-at-home mom, has the time to spend with her kids and do all the activities she wants with them. Susan triggers Samantha's Monger, who likes to remind Samantha that she is a bad mom.

Samantha finds herself talking about Susan because it makes her feel less crappy about herself. For the few minutes when Samantha is chatting with her neighbors about Susan, her Monger is quiet—but then inevitably as Samantha drives home her Monger fires up again.

Unfortunately, here's how the conversation usually goes:

"You are such a bitch. I can't believe you are so petty to go on and on about Susan's party last week.

How would you feel if people were judging you like that?" says her Monger.

Her BFF replies, "Oh, come on. Don't be such a goody two shoes. Everyone was doing it. It wasn't like you were the only one. They were all chatting about her and how her party was over the top. I mean who has the time to throw that kind of party. It was like Pinterest threw up all over it."

"Wow! You are so mean. I can't believe you are this mean about a stupid party. Susan is so nice and takes such good care of her kids. She is with them all the time. Unlike you who is always working late," shouts Samantha's Monger.

See how the Monger and BFF just go round and round, getting nowhere and not helping her feel any better? Enter the Biggest Fan:

When she notices her Monger chatting, Samantha simply pauses and says to herself, "Okay, I need to hear from my Biggest Fan." Sometimes that simple phrase helps remind her that the Monger isn't the only voice out there. It doesn't mean the Biggest Fan comes swooping in right away, but it does provide a pause for her to practice A.S.K.

Her Biggest Fan says, "Surprisingly, I have to agree with Ms. Monger. It's not that you are a bitch or mean, but the fact that you were talking about Susan so much is a red flag. What's really going on here? Slamming Susan might be a temporary relief, but overall it just makes you feel crappy because you are slamming another person, whom you call a friend. I get it that Susan triggers your insecurities around being a good mom. There is so much pressure to be the perfect mom. It gets overwhelming. So slamming how she spends her time makes you feel slightly better, but does it really? I think it just makes you feel worse. I mean why give the Monger any more fodder. Susan isn't perfect; I am sure she has her issues. Bashing Susan isn't going to make you a better mom."

A. (Acknowledge what you are feeling) It's okay to feel insecure, disappointed, and jealous.

S. (Slow down and get into your body) Stretch your hands above your head and slow down here.

K. (Kindly pull back to see the big picture) You are an awesome mom. How can you support yourself in your mothering? Maybe you need to be more intentional about spending time with your kids? Notice your unique talents at being a mom and where you want to make changes. Remember you need to stay in your own car here and just worry about you.

SOME STRAIGHT TALK

This is one of the hardest behaviors to unhook because drama and judging other people is everywhere in our society. Not only is there internal pressure from your Monger to engage in the behavior, there is pressure from your social circle. Recognizing this behavior and changing it took me a long time.

The biggest tip I have is to be honest. Notice how you feel about yourself after you talk about someone or engage in petty drama. Notice if it helps you feel better about yourself (if you are honest, it probably does momentarily). If over time it just makes you feel worse, be honest, acknowledge what is underneath your judgments. Be kind to yourself and make small steps towards change.

I Got This

Let's look at Samantha and her tendency to become a control freak. Does this sound familiar?

"I got this," Samantha says with a smile.

Her boss looks at her with a doubtful expression. "You can ask your team for help on this project, Samantha. You don't have to do it all. You are a manger for a reason."

"It's fine. I got it," Samantha replies as she hurries out the door.

Oh, my God, she thinks, my to-do list is a mile long! I am never going to get all this stuff done.

"Well then, you had better work harder and faster. If you don't do it, it won't get done right. Remember last year when you asked Todd to help and he totally dropped the ball. You can't rely on other people. Just keep plowing ahead!" her Monger says.

Samantha throws her stuff down in her office and makes a mad dash to grab some lunch, almost knocking over her co-worker Katie.

"Hey, I hear you are swamped, do you need some help? I can grab you lunch—I am on my way out," Katie says.

"Sure." Samantha reluctantly gives in, handing Katie $20 and saying, "I would love a turkey sandwich, no mayo on wheat, thank you so much."

"Okay, I will be right back!" says Katie and heads down the hall.

Thirty minutes later, Samantha is sitting at her computer trying to finish her part of the report. Katie drops the sandwich on her desk, "Sorry for the delay; it took longer than I thought."

"Thanks," Samantha mutters, barely looking up.

"No big deal, I am just *starving* over here. Doing *all* the work. It's just a simple sandwich, I mean how long can it take! I should have gone myself," mutters her BFF.

As Samantha opens her lunch, she sees a glop of mayo on the wrapper. Ugh! she thinks, I asked for no mayo.

"See, I *told* you! You can't trust anyone. You *have* to do everything yourself or it won't get done!" yells her Monger.

Raise your hand if you can relate to this scenario. This was totally me, and I see it in my clients all the time. The more stressed they get, the more control they seek. It is like the perfect match. Our Monger winds us up so much that we become consumed with being in control. When you notice yourself saying, "I got this" and thinking, I am so overwhelmed I don't know if I can do it all, take a step back.

Let's walk through that scenario with the Biggest Fan:

"I got this," Samantha says with a smile.

Her boss looks at her with a doubtful expression. "You can ask your team for help on this project, Samantha. You don't have to do it all. You are a manger for a reason."

"It's fine. I got it," Samantha replies as she hurries out the door.

Oh, my God, she thinks, my to-do list is a mile long! I am never going to get all this stuff done. Where is my Biggest Fan?

A. (Acknowledge what you are feeling) Whoa. You are totally overwhelmed. I get it. It is scary to ask for help, because what if they mess it up!? It brings up your insecurities too.

S. (Slow down and get into your body) Let's pause here in the office for 10 seconds and do a quick neck roll. Just take three deep breaths. You have a lot on your plate and your boss is suggesting you reach out for help.

K.(Kindly pull back to see the big picture) Maybe it is time to ask some co-workers for help. I know you hate asking for help, but help does not equal weakness. Help means you will be less stressed and a better worker, wife, and mother. Why don't you call a staff meeting for this afternoon and you can delegate some of these tasks?

Samantha's co-worker Katie offers to pick up a sandwich and returns with the dreaded mayo.

"Well that sucks. I hate mayo. She must have forgotten. Well I can either get a new sandwich or just scrape off the mayo. I will eat what I can and get some pretzels from the vending machine if I need more. In the scheme of things, this is *not* a big deal!"

Notice how her Biggest Fan could acknowledge what was really going on under all that panic. This acknowledgement allowed Samantha to slow down and look at options. The glitch comes when we acknowledge what we are feeling and then your Monger immediately jumps in with *you should* be doing more. Your Biggest Fan has your back. She will always steer you in the best direction for you. The challenging part is trusting her.

The other bonus was that once Samantha's Biggest Fan helped her see the power in delegating, everything else seemed far less stressful. The mayonnaise on her sandwich no longer felt like a 10 situation because she wasn't being attacked by her Monger. Samantha's overall stress dropped once she channeled her Biggest Fan. She was able to focus and she was more kind to herself and other people.

SOME STRAIGHT TALK

The "I got this" behavior is addicting. Being the go-to responsible person can feel so good—and it is exhausting. This behavior can feel like a straitjacket. It just keeps squeezing tighter and tighter. Recognizing the false high that "I got this" provides is so important.

Sometimes it is nice to be the responsible one. Enjoy those times. The problem is when the positive feelings morph into resentment and bitterness. Be honest with yourself. When you notice yourself saying, "I got this," check in and make sure you want to be handling everything or if you are doing it out of a sense of duty. It is all about being honest with your motivation and not making decisions from a place of should.

I DESERVE (ENTITLEMENT VS ACCOUNTABILITY)

The phrase "I deserve" is on this list not because it is a Monger phrase but because it is a BFF phrase, usually in response to a Monger attack or just a bad day. Regardless of the circumstances, it is a phrase that will come back to bite you in the ass later. You will act on something based on the "I deserve" justification only to have your Monger attack you for it later.

Your BFF encourages, "Go ahead. You had a really crappy day so you deserve to splurge on dessert."

Your Monger responds, "Yep, you totally deserved it, you fat ass. You have no self-control! So every time you have a bad day you are going to stuff your face? Sounds like a good plan to lose those extra 20 pounds!"

The phrase "I deserve" is a trap. It is a trap because it isn't a justification and it is usually a sign that you are doing something unconscious without thinking of the consequences.

You may need something or even want something, but when you say, "I deserve" it implies no ownership. It implies entitlement. When I hear myself say "I deserve," I quickly ask myself, Okay, do I want this? Do I need this? Or am I engaging in this activity for another purpose?

Frequently the phrase "I deserve" is a big fat middle finger to our Monger from our BFF.

Here's an example you might relate to:

> Your Monger has been hammering you all day about failing at work, missing the deadline for the school fundraiser, dropping the ball with dinner, etc. Your BFF says, "Screw it! Let's take care of ourselves. You deserve a cupcake! Hell, you deserve three cupcakes."
>
> (Let's be honest, we all know a cupcake isn't going to make the Monger be quiet, *and* it isn't going to make the issues of the day disappear.)
>
> "A cupcake! What is that going to do but make you fat. And three, puhleeze! You can't even cook a decent dinner and now you are going to eat cupcakes?" gripes your Monger.
>
> Rather than just rebelling against the Monger, take ownership of your behavior.
> - Do you want a cupcake? Think it through.
> - Would it taste good?
> - Do you want the extra sugar?
> - Is it worth the inevitable stomachache?
> - If your answer is yes, then eat a cupcake and relish every single bite.

The problem might come later if you decide to eat three cupcakes and your Monger chimes in, "Told you a cupcake wouldn't help. You are such a fat-ass, and now you are a fat ass with a stomach-ache. Nicely done!"

This is when you want to bring in your Biggest Fan. "Yep, I sure did eat three cupcakes!! I wanted three cupcakes and they tasted delicious, each and every bite. And yes, my stomach is *really* upset, so lesson learned for next time. No need to eat three. One would be fine. Maybe next time I will eat one and wait 15 minutes to see if I want another rather than eating all three back to back. "

When you take ownership of your behavior it isn't tied up in manipulation or secret shame. It is clear and proud. And if you make a decision that doesn't work out well, you can gather more facts for next time so you can keep making better and better decisions.

SOME STRAIGHT TALK

Okay, I admit this section sounds a little too good to be true, if not a little hokey. You might be reading it thinking, Yeah, yeah, yeah, I want the damn cupcake—back off. I want to be clear that I hear you and it is okay to have the damn cupcake and it is okay to eat as many as you like. The key here is being honest with yourself about what you are really doing. When you say, "I deserve" rather than "I want," you aren't being honest. You are falsely justifying something without really thinking it through, which is a trap of the BFF and ultimately the Monger. No, you don't have to give up your cupcakes. Yes, you have to be honest with yourself and own what it is you want.

SOLDIERING ON

Soldiering On is one of the most toxic behaviors in this chapter because it is held so proudly by so many people in our society and it leaves us exhausted, depleted, and stressed out.

Soldiering On is the idea that life is full of pain and suffering and therefore, if you are experiencing any pain and suffering, you should suck it up and keep moving. Our Monger *loves* Soldiering On.

Some common phrases that are used in Soldiering On include:

- "Never let them see you sweat."
- "Be grateful; it could be worse."
- "Think positive; it's not that bad."
- "Suck it up."
- "Be strong; don't burden other people with your problems."

Soldiering On is a necessary concept when used in short periods of great stress. There are times in our life when we do have to "suck it up" and keep moving forward, but when Soldiering On becomes a way of life, which I see happening all the time, it is a problem.

Let's revisit Samantha, who is caring for her two sons and her mom who has Alzheimer's.

Samantha is trying to do it all, and it often leaves her exhausted and tired at the end of the day.

Her Monger encourages her to Soldier On, "Ugh, this is so hard. But you should be positive; you have so many blessings. You could call Fran and vent but she has it so much worse caregiving for both her parents. You don't want to burden her. You need to just suck it up. Life is hard, and there is no sense whining about it. You have so much to do today and yes, it is overwhelming, but it could be worse. Count your blessings."

Soldiering On keeps Samantha stuck in overwhelm, pain, and exhaustion. It is not serving her; instead it is leaving her living in an isolated world of martyrdom and pain.

Now let's hear what happens when Samantha's Biggest Fan is in charge.

A. (Acknowledge what you are feeling) Ugh, this is so hard. You are exhausted! It is so terrifying being a caregiver. What if you forget something, what if something happens to your mom? You feel like you are dropping the ball all over the place. It is so scary to watch your mom fail and you can't help but think what if you get it someday. Are you going to burden your kids this way?

Her Biggest Fan encourages her to be honest with herself here—no Soldiering On, no sucking it up, no fixing it, just raw honesty that this situation is *hard*.

S. (Slow down and get into your body) Your head is throbbing, and you are exhausted. Your body is telling you that you need to rest. You are going to make it a priority tonight to go to bed early so you can read, relax and get a good night's sleep.

Her Biggest Fan draws attention to her body; because her body is telling Samantha she is too stressed. Her Biggest Fan knows that is a warning sign and that Samantha needs to take action.

K. (Kindly pull back to see the big picture) You have so much to do today it is overwhelming. Why don't you ask your husband to cook dinner tonight?

And you need to come up with a new plan for meal prep because it is just too much with your schedule. You are grateful for all he does and you know you can figure out a way to work this out differently. Why don't you call Fran on your way home from work? She is dealing with this too with her parents; she can understand what is happening. It is nice you have each other to lean on.

Samantha's Biggest Fan helps Samantha recognize she can't do it alone and realizes she needs to ask for help from her husband and other people too. She is willing to reach out to her friends, share her story, and get support. She understands that problems aren't graded. We all have problems. We all need support. Being vulnerable and reaching out isn't a weakness, it is a strength. Samantha's Biggest Fan leaves her more energized, less exhausted, and more connected to the world around her.

The toxic belief is that Soldiering On will gain us more productivity, more love, more respect. Soldiering On convinces us we have to do it alone, and we can't show any weakness.

Soldiering On is something that has been passed down through the generations and has become hard-wired into our lifestyles and our relationships. Learning to unhook it takes daily intention and a choice to not settle for our default patterns. But gradually over time, as your Biggest Fan's voice becomes louder, Soldiering On will no longer be a way of life.

I SHOULD FEEL

This was one of my mantras for a long time and when I hear clients say it I internally cringe. I *should* feel happy. I *should* feel blessed. I *shouldn't* feel sad, angry, scared, etc. The "I should" phrase is a favorite belittling phrase of the Monger because it shuts down any feelings. Our Monger *hates* feelings because they are so unknown and out of control.

We convince ourselves that if we tell ourselves to stop feeling something that the feeling will go away. We beat ourselves up for feeling a certain way (e.g., sad, angry, frustrated) or for not getting over it fast enough. Or we tell ourselves *what* we should feel (e.g., grateful, happy, content).

It doesn't matter what you *should* feel. The point is you *are* feeling something. And the sooner you acknowledge that feeling, the faster it might dissipate.

When we give ourselves permission to acknowledge the feeling, we can then do something about it. Here's an example:

> Your husband's family is visiting from Texas for the next two weeks and he wants to spend 24/7 with them! You love his family, but 24/7 is a lot of time with anyone let alone your in-laws.
>
> Your Monger reminds you, "You *should* be excited about seeing them. They came all the way from Texas just to visit you guys! Especially with all the time your husband spends with your family. You owe him. You should be more appreciative. They are so nice to you and you are just being ungrateful and bitchy."
>
> "Yes, but 24/7 is a bit much for family. Sure, your family lives here, but the beauty is you don't have to see them all the time. I get it that your husband wants to spend time with them but why should you? I bet if your family asked you to spend 24/7 with them he would say no way. You shouldn't have to do anything you don't want to do," says your BFF
>
> And then your Biggest Fan replies, "(*A. Acknowledge what you are feeling*) It's understandable that you would be dreading this visit. I know you love his family but 24/7 is a bit much. If you're honest, you aren't excited about spending that

much time with them. And that is okay. But you want to give your husband this gift of time with his family. (*S. Slow down and get into your body*) Take time to calmly sit down and discuss this situation with him. (*K. Kindly pull back to see the big picture*) Figure out how he can maximize his time and you can have a chance to bow out when you are feeling overwhelmed. Better to take care of yourself and admit you are going to get overwhelmed then end up resentful by the end of the two weeks."

Allowing your feelings to come up and be acknowledged allows them to diminish faster. When you *own* your feelings, you can find a way to deal with them that is healthier and more proactive. When we push the feelings down and allow our Monger to shame us into *not* feeling them, we become bitter and resentful.

CONCLUSION

When you can start noticing your favorite go-to behaviors, you will know when your Monger is running the show so you can implement A.S.K. that much faster.

The behaviors in this chapter are just some of the ones that show up when your Monger is running the show. As you start building more awareness of your Monger, you will start to recognize your favorite go-to behaviors and be able to personalize this process a little more.

Because the Monger is so wily, sometimes noticing these behaviors takes two seconds and sometimes, like Samantha, you have eaten a bag of chips and purchased $300 in clothing before you notice anything. That's okay. The key here is continuing to build awareness of your Monger and learning how to A.S.K. Now let's dive a little deeper into the A.S.K. process.

SOME STRAIGHT TALK

As you start noticing your Monger and BFF more, the temptation is to beat yourself up for them. Here's a common scenario: Your Monger starts in, "You are such a loser. I can't believe you are late yet again picking up your son from practice." OMG, you think, There I go again! I beat myself up all the time! I am such a loser! Why do I hammer myself so much? I am so bad at this self-compassion thing. See what happened there? You're beating yourself up for beating yourself up. It is so common and so natural, and that's why I'm bringing it up here.

As you start to notice your Monger more and more, remember to A.S.K. to hear from your Biggest Fan, who might say something like:

"Yep, you are running late again. You hate picking him up late because you feel like a bad mom, and like it makes him think you don't care. You just lost track of time. Slow down and notice the cars in front of you and take three slow breaths. You can explain to your son that you messed up and you are sorry. But beating yourself up for it isn't going to help. Obviously, you need to allow more time. Maybe you can set an alarm on your phone for when you need to leave the office and intentionally set it to go off a few minutes early."

Again, this is the hardest part of this process. Your Monger is wily and will always try to find a way to keep you from changing/growing purely because she gets scared with the unknown. So as you change and start to notice your Monger more and bring in the Biggest Fan more, your Monger will get nastier and trickier. All part of the process, my friend. All part of the process. Notice your Monger, A.S.K. to hear from your Biggest Fan, and move on.

CHAPTER SIX

A.S.K. Step 1: Acknowledge What You Are Feeling

As a reminder, here are the three steps to A.S.K. for your Biggest Fan's support:

Acknowledge what you are feeling: When your Monger tries to shame and belittle you, your Biggest Fan acknowledges what you are feeling (e.g., you must be tired, scared, angry, sad, etc.).

Slow down and get into your body: When your Monger tries to speed you up and make everything more intense, your Biggest Fan tries to slow everything down, encouraging you to take a break, pause, breathe, etc.

Kindly pull back to see the big picture: When your Monger just sees doom and gloom and engages in black-and-white thinking, your Biggest Fan sees lots of color. She encourages you to think of different solutions, brainstorm, and see the other colors. Most important, your Biggest Fan is *kind*. We tend to be harsh on ourselves when we are looking for new solutions, but it doesn't have to be that way.

THE F WORD

The first (and in my opinion the most important) part of channeling your Biggest Fan is to be honest with yourself and acknowledge what you are feeling. Trust me, I didn't always think that way, and if I could write a book about living happier and *not* include feelings, I would. One would think that because I am a counselor I would *love* everything about feelings. But no, I honestly think I went into counseling so I could rationalize myself out of my feelings.

After years of avoiding them, ignoring them, and intellectualizing them, I realized avoiding my feelings was leaving me more stressed and overwhelmed. My Monger (again that damn Monger!) spent a lot of time helping me avoid my feelings by creating drama, emotional eating, unnecessary conflicts, and so on. With my clients, I noticed that those who struggled with their Monger also struggled with acknowledging their feelings.

In her book *America the Anxious,* Ruth Whippman shares the theory that one of the root causes of anxiety is "a kind of institutionalized dishonesty that punishes people for experiencing a normal range of feelings."[1]

Yes! I agree this is a real problem in our society. Our quest for "happiness" has left us afraid of feeling anything but happiness. We aren't taught to acknowledge our feelings. In fact, we are taught to ignore them (especially the bad ones), so "soldier on" and "suck it up, Buttercup", become common mantras.

We look for happiness but we refuse to allow ourselves anger or sadness. And unfortunately, it doesn't work like that. We can't have one without the other.

Just like in the movie *Inside Out*[2] when Joy realizes that all the "happy" memories also had Sadness in them, all the emotions work together to make our lives rich and colorful.

Here's another story about Samantha as she throws her husband a surprise party.

> "Did you get the beer and wine?" Samantha yells into the speakerphone in her car. She's driving like a madwoman to pick up the cake for her husband's surprise 50th birthday party.
>
> "Yes," Her exasperated brother-in-law says.
>
> "Did you get some local breweries? He loves local breweries!"
>
> "Of course," he says.
>
> "What about standard Bud Light or Miller Lite? Not everyone is going to love local breweries!"
>
> "Yes, I have you covered. Trust me—the beer is handled."
>
> Samantha's best friend's face shows up on the screen and she hangs up with her brother-in-law with a quick thank you.
>
> Without saying hello, Samantha starts in with the questions for her friend. "How does the venue look? Do we have enough balloons? Do you think he will be surprised? What if someone ruins it? I am wigging out over here. There is so much to get done."
>
> Meanwhile in her head, Samantha's Monger is large and in charge: "You are never going to be able to pull this off. He is totally going to figure it out. You can't surprise him. You are going to feel so stupid when he tells everyone he already knew it was happening. What were you thinking doing a surprise party? You have way too much to do and you are so disorganized. This is going to be a complete failure."
>
> To avoid that awful Monger voice, Samantha spends all day running around like a woman on

speed trying to make sure everything is covered and taken care of (and driving all her friends crazy as well).

Samantha is stressed. Yes, planning a surprise party is stressful, and it's true she has a lot to do. However, her Monger is compounding her stress because her Monger doesn't want her to feel. Her feelings are unknown and scary, so to avoid them her Monger keeps her stuck in drama and perfectionism.

What is really going on here? Underneath all that drama and perfectionism, Samantha is scared. She is nervous that it won't go well. She is exhausted from running around all day (and probably needs a nap). She is feeling less than confident because her Monger is running the show. In a failed effort to not feel out of control with her feelings, she is creating more drama and stress for herself, thus feeling *more* out of control. Ironic, isn't it?

Here's how the cycle plays out:

- Samantha is nervous, scared about her husband's party (as anyone would be).
- Her Monger convinces her there is no time for her to feel anything, so she Soldiers On. And not only that, but her Monger tells her she is stupid and silly for feeling scared.
- Meanwhile, Samantha is getting more and more nervous and her anxiety is increasing, so Samantha lashes out at those closest to her.
- She becomes so anxious and disconnected from the party that she misses the whole thing because she is running around trying to make everything perfect. She isn't there for her husband. She is so stressed she can't eat any of the delicious food or even enjoy the local beer her brother-in-law bought.

This is why the Acknowledge step is *so* important. When we don't acknowledge our feelings, they come out in other places (stress, anxiety, perfectionism, hustling, etc.). They can and do cause physical symptoms like backaches, stomachaches, and headaches.

For so long we have heard that you must *feel your feelings,* as if it is some dramatic event. Once we *feel our feelings,* everything will be better. I always felt like I was missing something, though, because I didn't know how to feel my feelings. The biggest aha for me in discovering the A.S.K. process is that feeling my feelings starts with the simple step of Acknowledging what I am feeling.

In fact, simply acknowledging the existence of our feelings starts the ball rolling. I usually feel better simply because I was honest with myself for what is going on. I have spent so much of my life running from my feelings and making the situation a million times worse. Giving myself space to label the feelings and acknowledge their existence has made a world of difference. Trust me. I know it is uncomfortable, and I know it isn't something that we are taught to do. I know it goes against your instincts. I know your Monger hates it *and* it will help you reduce your stress and make you happier and more successful. I guarantee it. I have seen it in my own life and the lives of my clients (who were resistant to feeling anything negative).

You Can't Outrun Them:
Feelings Are Not Convenient but Are Relentless

"If you don't acknowledge it, then it isn't real" is a common belief. As if we have some control over our feelings and we can will ourselves to not feel anything negative!

Somewhere along the way we were taught our feelings are *bad* and we are to ignore them if they aren't convenient. We are taught that if you are feeling something negative, just don't think about it. In fact, just think positive. But researchers have found that theory just doesn't work. We can't think ourselves out of a feeling. In a 2012 study at Florida State University, researchers found that those who suppressed their negative thoughts more often had stronger stress responses than those who acknowledged the negative thoughts.[3]

The problem is our feelings are not always convenient. The part we missed in our education on feelings is that it isn't the *feeling* that is bad. It is our reaction to the feeling. Ironically, when we don't acknowledge a feeling is when it runs amok. We become angry about things that don't matter. We cry at sad movies rather than what is really troubling us. We yell at our kids about the dirty house rather than owning our frustration at our boss. We allow our Monger to drive us harder and faster to avoid the feelings rather than giving ourselves space to just feel the negativity. The moral of the story is you can't bypass your feelings; if you do, they will come back to bite you in the ass.

When it comes to acknowledging our feelings, Dr. Susan David, a psychologist at Harvard Medical School, writes in her book *Emotional Agility* that there tend to be two types of people: Brooders and Bottlers.[4]

> **Brooders:** They can't let it go. They are flooded by feelings. They tend to keep score of their hurts. Their intention is good. They want to feel happy, so they try to move beyond their negative feelings by thinking through their feelings and experiencing them fully over and over.

> **Bottlers:** Hold it all in, but it usually comes out in other places through misdirected feelings, physical ailments, or numbing. Their intention is good. They want to feel happy, so they try to move beyond their negative feelings by ignoring them and pushing them down.

In my experience, individuals who are overwhelmed by their Monger tend to fall on the Bottlers side of the continuum. They hold it in because they don't want to experience a lot of their negative feelings. They tell themselves the grief is too intense, the regret is too much, and the anger is too strong.

Feelings are messy. They bring up stuff. Stuff we don't want to experience. Here are the patterns that most Bottlers get stuck in.

Stuff it down: We tell ourselves it isn't appropriate to feel that way so we ignore it. Usually followed by some type of Numbing, Soldiering On, or Having a 10 Reaction to a 2 Situation as discussed in the previous chapter.

Analyze it: One of the ways our Monger tricks us into thinking we are "feeling the feeling" is to analyze it. We think we are helping because we are trying to understand ourselves. But when we immediately jump to the *why* without allowing the feeling, we get stuck in justifying, proving, and defending the feeling, which leads nowhere. Yes, the why is important eventually, but first we need to acknowledge the feeling and label it without defending it.

Judge it: Based on the *why* above, we move on to judging if it is okay that we are having the feeling; usually we decide it is not okay, so we circle back up to stuffing it.

Our feelings are actually pretty innocuous, so it is ironic we have spent much of our lives stuffing them down, trying to avoid them, or shaming ourselves for having them. Our feelings only last a certain period of time. In fact, Jill Bolte Taylor, a neuroanatomist and author of the *New York Times* best-selling memoir *My Stroke of Insight: A Brain Scientist's Personal Journey*, says our feelings only last 90 seconds. She explains our emotional response like this:

> "Once triggered, the chemical released by my brain surges through my body and I have a physiological experience. Within 90 seconds from the initial trigger, the chemical component of my anger has completely dissipated from my blood and my automatic response is over. If, however, I remain angry after those 90 seconds have passed, then it is because I have chosen to let that circuit continue to run."[5]

For those who are Brooders, this is helpful to know because it reminds you that if you are experiencing anger about a certain event for longer than 90 seconds it is probably because you choose to keep replaying the event in your brain and triggering the 90-second cycle every time.

And if you are a Bottler, this is helpful because you probably choose to not give yourself 90 seconds to feel the feeling. How often do you stop yourself from feeling something? You feel anger and within 30 seconds you say to yourself, "You shouldn't feel anger. Be grateful or be positive." So you stop the 90-second process. Later, your husband corrects you in front of a friend and you go off on him because you are so angry. Holding on to the feeling way too long because we never let it do its thing in our body cuts the feeling at its knees, which leaves us full of anxiety and stress.

Feelings are happening all the time. We see someone walking down the street towards us and we feel a certain way. Maybe we feel joyful or fearful. But the feeling only lasts a minute and then poof it is gone. The problem comes in when we judge our feelings, analyze them, and shove them back down because we decide they aren't worthy. When that judgment happens, we end up being punished for our feelings. The messy process is compounded.

Walking to meet her husband for a rare date night, Samantha sees her college boyfriend walking down the street holding hands with a beautiful woman. Immediately she feels excited to see him— and then a wave of jealousy washes over her.

"You shouldn't be feeling jealous! You are a happily married woman! Why do you care about *him*? You are so stupid. He broke your heart 25 years ago! Get over yourself," her Monger says.

Followed by her BFF: "Man, oh, man, doesn't he look good. Well you dodged a bullet with that one. He was such a jerk. Hold your head high, girlfriend. You lucked out with your husband. You guys have the perfect marriage."

"Well, I wonder what your life would be like if you were with him? Maybe he is the one that got away. I mean your man is great, but is he really?! Look how cute your ex is and he looks successful too. But you weren't good enough for him in college. No wonder he rejected you."

"*Please*. He didn't reject you! You rejected him. And for good reason, he was a J-E-R-K," her BFF says with a laugh.

And back and forth they go.

By the time, Samantha sees her husband, she has hammered herself into a bloody pulp and her BFF and Monger have gone 10 rounds. She is feeling a mix of shame and sadness. She spends much of the night in silence, too far in her head to listen to her husband, who then thinks she is mad at him. To say the least, date night was ruined.

See how that works? Samantha had a feeling but she did not feel it, she intellectualized it, and made herself feel bad for having it in the first place. Let's try that again.

> Walking to meet her husband for a rare date night, Samantha sees her college boyfriend walking down the street holding hands with a beautiful woman. Immediately she feels excited to see him and then a wave of jealousy washes over her.
>
> Wow! (*A. Acknowledge what you are feeling*) He looks good. Funny how you can still be excited to see him after all these years. Makes sense. I mean you dated him for what, three years?! That is a long time. It is natural to feel excited and jealous. Look at that woman he is with. She is so cute. I hope they are happy. You can't help but be jealous. He rejected you so of course you are going to be jealous! Doesn't mean you don't love your husband and your life. It's just old feelings.
>
> By the time, Samantha meets up with her husband, she has taken three deep breaths and is feeling calm and relaxed. She allowed herself the 90 seconds and she even shares with him that she saw an ex from college walking down the street. They have a wonderful time laughing and talking. A couple times throughout the night she has flashbacks to seeing her ex walking down the street and she notices that feeling and takes a deep breath. By the end of the night she realizes she and her husband have had an amazing date night. She is so thankful that they are together, building their future.

True, sometimes we feel things on a deeper level than just seeing an ex. Sometimes we are dealing with loss or grief or depression. And it works the same way. When those feelings come up and we acknowledge them, welcome them, and own what we are experiencing without judgment, they can pass through with ease and we can move on to the next thing in our lives.

LABEL IT

Just label it. I am feeling tired, scared, sad, hungry, anxious, nervous, happy, joyful, vulnerable.

A. Acknowledge what you are feeling means label the feeling. Once you identify and acknowledge what you are feeling, you can move to the second step, S. Slow down and get into your body.

SOME STRAIGHT TALK

As you are reading this, pay attention to your Monger. I bet she is telling you, "This is stupid. Label your feelings, yeah, yeah, yeah." Remember what I said about your Monger being wily. The hardest part about doing this work is that our Monger works against us. Your Monger hates change and will convince you that anything that involves changing how you have always done it is wrong. This "feeling your feelings" thing is going to be especially troubling to your Monger, so the resistance is all part of the process.

At first, because your Monger is so judgmental of feeling, it might be easier to notice the physical sensations caused by the feeling. For years, I would notice physical sensation (e.g., my neck is tight, my head hurts, my stomach is growling, my eyes won't stay open, etc.) before I would notice the feeling. When you notice the physical sensation simply ask yourself, What am I feeling?

Getting in the practice of acknowledging it will take some time, but it is key. This step might be the only one you practice for a while. That's okay. It is an important step, so even if you can only practice the A. in A.S.K., it will still quiet your Monger and bring in your Biggest Fan.

Give yourself permission to just label whatever is coming up. Not having a reaction to it, not having to act. Just notice it. Frequently when we give ourselves permission to just label the feeling and allow it to have a presence, it will dissipate. Here's a story from Samantha's life that I'm sure you can relate to:

> Samantha wakes up feeling tired.
>
> "You shouldn't feel tired; I mean you slept for seven hours! How much sleep do you need?! You are so lazy. Get it together. Power through. You have a lot to do today," her Monger reminds her.
>
> You're right, Samantha thinks, I shouldn't be tired. What is my problem?! Samantha drinks an extra cup of coffee to help her power through. No rest for the weary, she sighs, and heads out the door to drop the kids at soccer practice.
>
> On her way home, Samantha drives through Starbucks for another cup of coffee. "You deserve it. You are tired and just need a boost. Your husband was snoring all night so of course you didn't sleep well. But you have to make it through the day, so a little caffeine is just what you need!" cheers her BFF.
>
> By early afternoon, Samantha's stomach is killing her. Too much coffee, she thinks. I've gotten a lot done, but man am I jittery.
>
> "That's the price you pay for being so lazy. We still have more to accomplish today if you want to be a winner. Keep moving," says her Monger.

As Samantha heads out to pick up the kids from practice, she swings by McDonald's for a Diet Coke. Her coffee buzz has worn off and she just needs a little kick to get through the afternoon. When the kids get in the car, chatting loudly and excited from practice, Samantha snaps at them for being too loud. She is exhausted and *done*. But there is still much to do.

At 5 o'clock, Samantha's anxiety is through the roof and she can't wait to have a glass of wine to take the edge off. "You deserve it. It has been a hell of a day," says her BFF.

Here's version 2.0 where Samantha owns her feelings:

Samantha wakes up feeling tired.

"You shouldn't feel tired; I mean you slept for seven hours! How much sleep do you need?! You are so lazy. Get it together. Power through. You have a lot to do today," her Monger reminds her.

Then her Biggest Fan chimes in. "Well it doesn't really matter if you should or shouldn't be tired, you *are* tired. Isn't that the point? Why do you need to justify tired? Bottom line, if you are tired, you need to take a nap. You aren't going to shame yourself out of being tired. Maybe when you get home from dropping the kids you can take a quick power nap."Samantha takes a big exhale, already feeling better.

After dropping the kids at soccer, Samantha sets her alarm for a 15-minute power nap. Her Monger chimes in, "We have stuff to do! What are you doing? We have no time for a nap, come on!" "Just back off, Monger lady. If you sleep for 15 minutes now you will feel better for the rest of the day." Her Biggest Fan has her back.

Samantha closes her eyes, and when her phone alarm beeps she wakes up ready to check things off her list. When she gets tired throughout the day she pauses, takes a deep breath, touches her toes, and checks in with herself.

At 9 pm, Samantha says to her husband, "I'm headed to bed. I didn't sleep well last night and I'm tired."

"Okay, love you," he says. "I hope you sleep better tonight."

As Samantha makes her way upstairs, her Monger chimes in. "What are you, 10 years old? A 9 pm bedtime!? You have so much to get done."

"Yep, it is time to catch up on your sleep. The to-do list will be equally long tomorrow and you will feel better if you just get some sleep," says her Biggest Fan.

Researchers at UCLA found that people have the belief that if they name the feeling they will feel worse.[6] But in additional studies, they found that when we use one or two words to own the feeling, we have less of a biological response.[7] The key is in the labeling.

Many of my clients who are Bottlers live in fear of becoming a Brooder. They think that if they own one of their feelings that makes them super needy and a wallower. Here's the reality for all you Bottlers out there: the danger of you becoming a Brooder because you start labeling your feelings is highly unlikely. We are less likely to get stuck in the feeling when we label it. We get stuck in the feeling when we start obsessing about the why and justifying if it is okay to have the feeling. That justification often leads to drama and Having a 10 Reaction to a 2 Situation. When we label the feelings, we allow ourselves the 90 seconds and it is over. That is it. Nothing mysterious or crazy.

Let's revisit Samantha and her husband's surprise 50th birthday party. In this version of the story, she is trying to not let her Monger run the show today and channel her Biggest Fan more. But it is a process that doesn't always go perfectly.

Samantha wakes up stressed. Today is the big day! She has been preparing for this party for weeks now and she can't believe it is here.

As Samantha steps into the shower, she takes a deep breath and reminds herself to simply *be* in the shower. While she shampoos and conditions, her thoughts keep heading to her to-do list. It's okay. I got this. I have a great team. We are going to have fun. The whole point of this day is to celebrate my husband, not get it perfect.

Samantha sets an alarm on her phone to go off every 60 minutes to remind her to breathe and keep coming back to the big picture, which is celebrating her husband, *not* planning a perfect party.

Later that morning Samantha's Monger is getting louder and louder, reminding her that every detail needs to be perfect. As she is chatting with her brother-in-law, her overwhelm sneaks out and she Has a 10 Reaction to a 2 Situation. Notice how she catches herself.

"Did you get the beer and wine?" Samantha yells into the speakerphone in her car. She's driving like a madwoman to pick up the cake for the party.

"Yes," her exasperated brother-in-law says into the phone.

"Did you get some local breweries? He loves local breweries!"

"Of course," he says.

"What about standard Bud Light or Miller Lite? I mean, not everyone is going to love local breweries, right?"

"Yes, I have you covered. Trust me—the beer is handled," Mark replies with an exasperated sigh.

Samantha hears his sigh and reminds herself to breathe. She is getting caught up in perfection and taking it out on her brother-in-law. She remembers she has to Acknowledge what she is feeling.

"Okay, Mark, I'm sorry, I'm just so stressed that everything isn't going to go well. I am trying to stay focused on the big picture, that it is about celebrating Steve's 50th, not getting it perfect."

Mark laughs knowingly in the phone, "We have your back. Steve is going to love it and everyone will have a good time! Trust me. Take a breath. We got this!"

"Thanks for all your help! I couldn't do this without you," says Samantha.

Samantha hangs up and puts on her favorite song to sing along to as she drives to pick up the cake. She has to call her best friend to check in but that can wait. She needs a few minutes to just decompress.

When her husband finally arrives at the party with his best friend he is grinning ear to ear. She doesn't miss a moment as he grabs her and hugs her. Throughout the night, she can hear his laugh and each time she smiles. Later that night as they are driving home and recapping all the festivities, he grabs her hand and says, "Thank you, that was an amazing surprise. I can't believe you pulled it off!" Samantha breathes in the moment and reminds herself that *this* is what is most important. Not the beer or the details but her relationship with her husband. And for once, her Monger is silent.

Acknowledging your feelings is a process. Owning that you are feeling something after years of pushing it down and avoiding it takes time. So make sure to give yourself a break as you work through this step.

When we have spent our whole lives avoiding our feelings, being able to identify them and label them is like learning a foreign language. On the following page is a chart that lists feelings and their intensities. Use this as a way to get in touch with what you are feeling. Initially, you can just identify with one of the basic emotions at the top and then try to drill down and get more specific. When you first start labeling your feelings, everything feels like it is a high intensity because you are so uncomfortable with feelings in general. For example, you might say "I feel angry" because you are so uncomfortable with anger that everything feels like seething, but in reality you might be just annoyed. There is a big difference between feeling seething and feeling annoyed. Recognizing the intensities and knowing that not all feelings are high intensity is helpful in making us more comfortable with feelings overall.

CONCLUSION

Acknowledging your feelings is the first step in channeling your Biggest Fan—and one of the hardest. Give yourself lots of time and room with this step. Your Monger is not comfortable with feelings and will give you *a lot* of pushback. That is okay and to be expected.

As you hear your Monger chatting, practice A.S.K. Acknowledge that this process is uncomfortable.

Own that it is stretching you.

Label that it makes you want to crawl out of your skin. Our Monger loves to distract us from the truth in our life. The more you can acknowledge what is really going on, the better you will feel.

Labeling: What Are You Feeling?

	Happy	Sad	Angry	Afraid	Ashamed
High Intensity	Excited	Hurt	Outraged	Alarmed	Remorseful
	Elated	Hopeless	Furious	Panicky	Worthless
	Overjoyed	Sorrowful	Seething	Suspicious	Disgraced
	Thrilled	Depressed	Enraged	Frantic	Powerless
	Exuberant	Alone	Irate	Horrified	Inferior
	Ecstatic	Unwanted	Betrayed	Petrified	Mortified
	Passionate	Miserable	Jealous	Shocked	Helpless
Medium Intensity	Cheerful	Heartbroken	Upset	Insecure	Apologetic
	Thankful	Somber	Frustrated	Uneasy	Unworthy
	Good	Distressed	Agitated	Frightened	Sneaky
	Hopeful	Lost	Disgusted	Threatened	Guilty
	Relieved	Melancholy	Defensive	Intimidated	Embarrassed
Low Intensity	Glad	Unhappy	Annoyed	Cautious	Bashful
	Content	Moody	Uptight	Nervous	Secretive
	Pleasant	Blue	Resistant	Worried	Regretful
	Mellow	Gloomy	Touchy	Unsure	Uncomfortable
	Pleased	Disappointed	Irritated	Apprehensive	Pitied
	Satisfied	Dissatisfied	Tense	Timid	Silly

To print this handout visit:
http://live-happier.com/the-happier-approach-giveaways/

CHAPTER SEVEN

A.S.K. Step 2: Slow Down and Get into Your Body

Once you acknowledge what you are feeling, the next step is slowing down and getting into your body.

Okay, here's the truth. To deal with the Monger, you *have* to get out of your head and get into your body. Most of us live mostly in our head. We literally aren't even aware that we have a body unless it starts to hurt, and then we just take a pill to make it better. Our Monger takes up a lot of space in our head. So the more time we spend in our head, the more we stay out of our body and the louder our Monger gets.

One key to channeling your Biggest Fan is getting into your body. When we can slow down and get into our body, we change our perspective. By changing our physical presence, we can see more options and the last step, K. Kindly pull back to see the big picture, happens with more ease.

When I share this step with my clients, their eyes glaze over and I can almost hear them internally saying, Yeah, yeah, yeah, get into your body. Thanks to more and more research being done on the mind-body connection,[1] we have heard so many times that we need to slow down and get into our bodies that we don't even hear it anymore. And I know that when you are in go-go-go mode, checking off the to-do list and running from activity to activity, the *last* thing you want to do is get into your body. Trust me. I get it.

I fought for years the idea of getting out of my head and into my body. Whenever you hear the words "get into your body," the next word you often hear is "meditate." Meditation is awesome if you are able to meditate and/or have a regular meditation practice. Rock on. You can use that practice with the second step of A.S.K., S. Slow down and get into your body.

A meditation practice is amazing, and meditation is not for everyone. Honestly, I couldn't meditate for five minutes even if you held a gun to my head! For way too many years I beat myself up for the fact that I couldn't meditate. My Monger convinced me that there was only one way to get into your body and it was through meditation. So if I couldn't meditate, I would never be able to slow down and be present. (See how wily the Monger can be?!)

Finally, I accepted that I was not going to be a super meditator (or even an average meditator) and I tried to find a way to hack it. No, I don't do 30 minutes of meditation a day or even five minutes. More like 10 seconds. I realized that even if I just touched my toes or wiggled my body for a few seconds and took some deep breaths while doing it, I was able to shift out of the headspace of the Monger.

Amy Cuddy's book *Presence* describes how changing your body position and holding a power pose can change your mindset: "Expanding your body language—through posture, movement, and speech—makes you feel more confident and powerful, less anxious and self-absorbed, and generally more positive."[2]

Simply changing your physical state can shift your mindset. I encourage my clients (and myself) to take 10–20 seconds to change their physical state. I call these brief breaks Mindfulness Hacks.

MINDFULNESS HACKS EXAMPLES

Wiggle your body
Dance to your favorite song
Touch your toes
Reach for the sky
Roll your neck
Sit up straight
Take three deep breaths at a stoplight
Be in the shower
Drink a glass of water slowly
Check in with your five senses: what do I see, hear, taste, smell, and feel?
Feel your feet on the ground
Notice the sky
Notice the trees

Mindfulness Hacks are simple and quick ways to slow down and get into our body. They work in two ways: Action and Prevention.

Action: This is the S. part of A.S.K. When you notice your Monger chatting or one of the behaviors that indicate your Monger is running the show, practice a 10-second Mindfulness Hack. This allows you to get out of your head and into your body and to channel your Biggest Fan. One of my favorite practices for this one is to literally wiggle my body, because it makes me laugh and also because it changes my perspective and reminds me to literally give myself some wiggle room. But it doesn't have to be that dramatic. I encourage clients to choose several go-to Mindfulness Hacks such as taking three deep breaths, feeling your feet on the floor, touching your thumb to your fingers, doing a neck roll, or stretching.

Prevention: You can also use Mindfulness Hacks to cultivate more awareness of your Monger. Randomly throughout the day, do a quick movement that puts you in your body: touch your toes, look up and notice the clouds, or take three deep breaths at a stoplight. These Mindfulness Hacks help break the endless chatter of your mind (aka your Monger) and allow you to spend some time in your body (and with your Biggest Fan). Your Monger tends to lull you into a trance of being critical and shaming. Because these Mindfulness Hacks pull you out of your mind and change your physical state, you can start to break that trance and notice your Monger chatting. The more you can break the Monger trance, the less power your Monger will have.

Here are some examples of how Samantha uses Mindfulness Hacks to Slow down and get into her body:

Action: Samantha has an afternoon of errand running. She always hates running errands but today her to-do list is exceptionally long. Part of why she hates errands is that her Monger is exceptionally loud, hammering her about efficiency and doing it right. It is exhausting!

As she stands in the long line at Target, her Monger chimes in, "You picked the wrong lane. Why did you think it would be a good idea to come to the store on Saturday afternoon? You should have picked a different time."

Samantha takes a few deep breaths and slowly she touches her thumb to her fingers.

"This is the only time you could come this week. It's no big deal. Pick one of your favorite magazines and read it while you are waiting in line. Maybe you could put on your headphones and listen to some of your favorite music," her Biggest Fan says.

Prevention: When Samantha is running errands, she tries to park at the back of the lot. As she walks to the store she takes deep breaths and pays attention to her feet touching the ground.

She hears from her Biggest Fan: "There is no hurry here; we have all day. We have to do this anyway, might as well enjoy it."

CONCLUSION

Slowing down and getting into your body is a key step because it changes our physical perspective. We are so often in go-go-go mode, where our Monger chats unchecked. Pulling ourselves out of that mode to slow down and get into our body is challenging, which is why the Mindfulness Hacks work so well. Pick a few of your favorites and put them on sticky notes around your house or set an alarm on your phone to remind you to practice one of them. When you do the S. Slow down and get into your body step, you can literally shut out the continual blah blah blah of the Monger as you concentrate on what is going on in your body. Which then allows the next step, K. Kindly pull back to see the big picture, to flow that much easier.

SOME STRAIGHT TALK

A couple of years ago I started posting these Mindfulness Hacks in my newsletter. I included random exercises such as the ones I describe above—touch your toes or wiggle your body—and encouraged people to take these 10-second breaks. But in all honesty, I wasn't doing them myself. I *knew* the importance of them but I wasn't practicing them.

Until I decided to challenge myself to practice what I preach. Each week I developed a new way to get into your body, a new Mindfulness Hack. I challenged people to join me in doing it and I posted myself practicing on social media to make myself accountable (and as a bonus, market my business). To be honest, marketing my business was more of the initial draw than the actual getting into my body. But wow, was I blown away by the results.

Much to my surprise, I discovered that this getting into your body thing really works! I practiced both Prevention and Action, so when I heard my Monger chatting I practiced the Mindfulness Hack of the week to channel my Biggest Fan. And I also practiced the Mindfulness Hack randomly for 10 seconds at a time throughout the day as prevention against my Monger. Amazingly, my Monger became less powerful because I was more aware of her. I used to spend much of my day having her chat away unnoticed. When I started practicing these Mindfulness Hacks, I noticed her chatting sooner and could channel my Biggest Fan. As I practiced it more and more every time I did a Mindfulness Hack, my Biggest Fan naturally began to show up and I had regular visits from her throughout the day. It was a game changer for sure. And now I am a true believer in regularly getting into your body.

CHAPTER EIGHT

A.S.K. Step 3: Kindly Pull Back to See the Big Picture

After you have Acknowledged your feelings, and Slowed down and gotten into your body, it is time to Kindly pull back to see the big picture. The key part of this is *kindly*. Too often when we pull back, we get lost in a sea of judgment. Our Monger tells us, "You are doing it wrong," "You will fail," "There are too many options." We get wrapped up in justifying or proving why we are feeling a certain way. So when we pull back *kindly* we are giving ourselves lots of love and wisdom. Pulling back kindly and being open to all the options allows us to move beyond the traps of the Monger and find solutions that will move us forward.

This last step is where the Biggest Fan shows her kindness and wisdom. So what does this look like, you might be wondering? Here are some signs:

1. Our Biggest Fan doesn't use shame and belittling when looking at options. There is no "should" or "other people do it" in her vocabulary.

2. She always has our best interests at heart. She is kind, not judgmental, and she doesn't lead us down a path that will hurt us eventually (like our BFF might).

Throughout this chapter, I will be discussing the ways our Biggest Fan show us the big picture in a kinder, more helpful way than our BFF or Monger.

THE BIG PICTURE

Here's another example from Samantha's life where she practices Step 3 of A.S.K., K. Kindly pull back to see the big picture:

Samantha's son announces that he needs to bring something to the school bake sale tomorrow. She thinks to herself, Okay, I will have to swing by the store and pick something up. Then her son chimes in with, "I was hoping you could make your famous coconut cake. It is *so* good and I have already told the other kids you were making it. Maybe I can help you make it tonight?!"

Immediately she thinks to herself, Ugh, I don't have time to make the coconut cake. That will take at least three hours. I am already exhausted and now I have to make a freakin' coconut cake, too!

"You are such a terrible mom. Come on, he doesn't ask for much; the least you can do is make the coconut cake. Just stay up later and do it. He deserves it. You want to maintain 'favorite mom' status, don't you? If you don't make the cake, then he will hate you as a mom," says Samantha's Monger.

"No way, you don't have time to make the coconut cake. And that is okay, lady. He has a great life and he might be disappointed but you have to take care of you. He can't always get his way, plus he totally told you last minute. How are you supposed to make a coconut cake when you didn't even know it is happening?! You have to put your foot down and be a hard-ass sometimes. Why should you lose sleep over a bake sale cake? Give me a break. Go to the store. Buy a cake and be done with it," snaps her BFF.

To which her Monger replies, "It's a bake sale. You can't show up there with a store-bought cake! That is so tacky."

This war between the BFF and Monger goes on all day. Later, Samantha snaps at her husband when he asks if there is anything going on that night (a 10 Reaction to a 2 Situation). And she realizes, Wait a minute, where is my Biggest Fan here? So she A.S.K.s to hear from her and she replies,

"Ugh! I get it, this just sucks. You feel like a terrible mom if you disappoint him. Pause and do a little wiggle. It is so hard because you don't want to disappoint him, and yet you could wring his neck for telling you so last minute!! But this isn't an all-or-nothing thing.

"Here are the facts:

1. Your son wants you to bring a coconut cake,
2. He told you last minute,
3. He wants to help you make it,
4. You don't want to disappoint him, and
5. You are already exhausted.

"Let's think about this for a minute. What is the big picture here? What really matters? That your son feels loved and appreciated and you aren't up all night making a cake. What if you told him you can't make the coconut cake from scratch but you can make something from a box. You could go to the store and he can help you pick out a box dessert to make together. And then you can make the coconut cake next month for his grandma's birthday.

"Lots of options there. Yes, your son might still be disappointed, but he will regroup and figure it out. You are teaching him resilience and that life isn't always the way you expect it to be."

By pulling back and looking at the big picture, your Biggest Fan can help you see other options and not get stuck in just looking at the black and white of it all. As a reminder, be wary of those if-then statements (e.g., *If* I don't make the coconut cake *then* I am a terrible mom). Your Monger *loves* if-then statements, because they keep you stuck in all-or-nothing thinking. That is why this step must be done kindly, because our Monger doesn't like options. We have to be extra kind to ourselves as we look at the big picture.

Special Tip: Brainstorming

When you notice the war between the BFF and the Monger, pull back and A.S.K. yourself, What is the big picture here? Let me brainstorm some ideas. Remind yourself that all ideas are useful. You aren't going to use all of them, but they are useful. It is helpful just knowing we have choices.

SEEING OTHER COLORS

Our Monger forces us to look at the world in black and white, where there is a *right way* and a *wrong way* to do everything. This is why we are so attracted to the idea of finding the right way. Yes, our Monger has consistently told us the lie that there is a right way. When our Monger and BFF argue, we are simply moving between one extreme and the other. Luckily, our Biggest Fan sees the other colors and lives in the middle world where happier stress-free options are available.

Special Tip: Using the *And*

Using the word *and* is the most powerful way I have found to expand beyond the two extremes. *And* allows you to take two opposing ideas and make them one thought. I want to work out *and* right now I am tired. Both are true. I want to eat an ice cream sundae *and* I know ice cream upsets my stomach. Both are true.

Here's an example of how Samantha started using the *and* in her life.

Samantha flops onto the sofa, remote in hand. She is thrilled to have a Saturday evening with no plans. Just she and her husband, comfy clothes, cold beverages, and their favorite TV shows.

Just then, Samantha's husband comes in from working in the yard. "Hey, Mindy from next door invited us over for a last-minute neighborhood barbecue."

"No," Samantha sighs. "I just want to hang at home tonight."

"Okay," he says, "I thought it would be fun, but if you want to say no that's okay. I mean it isn't often we have time to hang with the neighbors, so I thought it would be cool to take advantage of the timing, but I get it. You look comfy, so let me call Mindy and then I can change clothes and join you on the couch."

Then she hears from her Monger, "Come on, get it together. You are so anti-social. You should be jumping at the chance to hang with the neighbors. I can't believe you are going to be such a lump on the couch. You should take advantage of the invite when you get it. And you are keeping your husband down too."

And then her BFF, "You deserve a night off. Don't worry about the neighbors. They are so loud anyway. You don't have to feel bad. Just enjoy yourself."

Enter the Biggest Fan. "It's okay to want a Saturday night off. That does not mean you are anti-social or a terrible neighbor. It means you are tired. Let's take a deep breath.

"Okay, there are options here.

- You enjoy being social *and* you don't want to go out tonight.
- You love your neighbors *and* you are tired.
- Your husband can support you *and* go hang with the neighbors.
- You could skip the dinner part and hang at home *and* join them after dinner for a drink or two.
- You could go for dinner *and* come home immediately and hit the couch.
- You could say no to tonight *and* make sure you schedule something for later."

Get in the habit of asking yourself, Where is the *and* here?

FORGIVENESS

Our Biggest Fan offers us forgiveness, while our Monger offers us shame and our BFF offers us justification.

Forgiveness allows us to move on, make changes, and grow. Without forgiveness, we are stagnant.

Let's revisit Samantha the morning after she had too much to drink with friends, when her hangover prevented her workout. Here's how the three voices weighed in:

Monger: "Way to go! You are such a lush. You can't say no, can you. You have no self-control and now you are miserable and fat. You are never going to get in shape. Wow! You can't do anything right. You can't keep your word and you are a miserable alcoholic. Hope it was worth it! You have to sit all day and watch soccer games. That is going to be miserable. And what will all the other moms say when they see you? They will totally know you are hung-over."

BFF: "Don't be such a party pooper. I mean you had fun, right!? It was totally worth it because it was such a terrible day. You deserved to let loose and party with Megan! It was a blast and you will remember that night way more than you will remember being home early so you could work out today. It's just one night and it was well worth it. Tell your kids you're sick! They won't know the difference."

Biggest Fan: "Hangovers are the worst! It sucks to feel so awful. I get it you are tired! Let's just lie here for a minute and breathe. You did have fun, and you would have had fun with two drinks rather than four. Next time we will remember that. This working out thing is important to you and sticking by your goals/intentions is new, so we will do better next time. Drink some fluids, eat a good breakfast, and maybe this afternoon you will feel up to working out."

Notice how her Biggest Fan acknowledges where Samantha is and the gap that exists between that and where she wants to be. Her Monger points to the gap using judgment or shame. And her BFF ignores the gap. The Biggest Fan acknowledges the gap and offers Samantha forgiveness, *then* she moves on to the next trait, curiosity.

CURIOSITY

The Biggest Fan is always encouraging you to be curious. She sees everything as an experiment. There is no judgment. Right and wrong don't exist. Every situation offers a chance to provide more wisdom.

Curiosity is a key part to K. Kindly pull back to see the big picture. Too often, our Monger steps in and uses curiosity as a way to be judgmental. The question isn't "Why did this happen?" (which leads to more judgment and shame), it's "What could I do differently? How can I improve the outcome?" Asking these questions allows you to come up with new ideas and options.

Here are some situations where curiosity is key. Notice how the Monger, BFF, and Biggest Fan Kindly pull back to see the big picture (or not!).

You just found out you lost your job.

Monger's Response: Why did you lose your job? Why did you get fired? Why did you make that choice that led to them firing you? Why are you so incompetent?

Notice how judgmental those questions are. They keep you stuck in justification and analysis paralysis.

BFF's Response: How could your boss fire you? How can you make him pay? Is there anything you can take from the office, without getting caught?

The BFF has your back, and she keeps you stuck in blame of others. There are no future options; it is all about keeping score in the present.

Biggest Fan's Response: What do you need to change moving forward? What other jobs might you enjoy? Whom do you need to talk to about finding another job? How long can you go without a job?

These questions provide you with options to move forward. They help you critically look at the situation and see next steps without judgment and shame.

You fight with your spouse about household chores.

Monger's Response: Why do you always pick a fight with him? Why are you so touchy about the chores anyway? You *should* be able to handle this stuff.

Judgment, judgment, and more judgment.

BFF's Response: He is so lazy! I mean seriously. What more could you do? You do it all. And when he tries to pitch in he usually does it wrong anyway.

Blame, blame, blame.

Biggest Fan's Response: What could be different? What do you need to change to make the situation better? What does he need to change to make this better? Is this fight really about the chores? What else might be going on? Is there something you need that you are too afraid to ask for?

The Biggest Fan doesn't get stuck in judgment, which inevitably leads to shame and belittling. She lives in curiosity not blame.

Here are some questions you can ask.

Practice saying to yourself, Hmmm, so that just happened. This creates some distance between you and what happened. Then ask:

- What are the *facts* in this situation?
- How can this situation improve?
- What am I in control of?
- What do I need to change to see it differently?
- What do I need to accept about myself to move forward?
- What assumptions am I making?
- What additional information do I need?
- What questions or clarifications might help?

Getting curious allows room for growth and change as well as the opportunity for more wisdom.

CONCLUSION

This final step in the process is what separates out the voice of the Biggest Fan from the Monger and BFF. Because our Monger keeps us stuck in a tunnel of absolute thinking, we have blinders on to any other options. The first two steps, A. Acknowledge what you are feeling and S. Slow down and get into your body, allow us to give ourselves empathy and get into our bodies long enough so we can pull those blinders off and do the final step. During this final step, we can look around and see all we have missed. We can see all the choices and options we have. If we jump to this step immediately, we might not have our blinders completely removed. We might still be blinded by the Monger, so the options and choices we brainstorm won't be as varied.

Make it a game. See how many options you can brainstorm. As you limit the judgments in your head, you will be amazed how many ways you can solve a problem.

SOME STRAIGHT TALK

A.S.K. is the overall process I teach to help my clients get in touch with their Biggest Fan. It encompasses the three concepts I have found work the best to quiet the Monger. I teach them and use them in the order I present.

However, I encourage you to make A.S.K. your own. The people I work with who have the greatest success with quieting their Monger tweak this process to best serve their individual needs. Some clients do the process exactly as I describe but they have specific ways they do each step that they have found work best for them. Others find doing S. Slow down and get into your body first works best.

I also have clients who, after years of doing this process, find that depending on the situation they can shortcut and jump right to K. Kindly pull back to see the big picture. Notice I said after YEARS of practice and depending on the subject. I know your temptation will be to shortcut to K. Kindly pull back to see the big picture every time. But you must—and I do mean must—master the first two steps (A. Acknowledge what you are feeling and S. Slow down and get into your body) first. You have to get comfortable acknowledging your feelings and getting into your body.

I, for one, practice A.S.K. pretty much in full every time. I find when I try to skip to K. Kindly pull back to see the big picture, I eventually pay the price later because I have skipped over the biggest step for me (feelings). So my message is make it your own, personalize it so it fits your life, and initially implement all the steps no matter how uncomfortable it is.

CHAPTER NINE

What's Most Important to You?

In the beginning of the book, I talked about how the Monger
encourages us to strive for external markers and how that constant push to do what we "should" do leaves us feeling empty
and exhausted. Frequently, after my clients and I have walked
through the process of quieting their Monger, there is a sense of
what happens now? They have spent their whole lives following
the goals of the Monger (perfectionism, people pleasing, or
staying small), so when the Monger isn't in charge anymore
they ask, What am I striving for now?

In this chapter, we are going to turn the focus inward. We
are going to name what is most important to *you* and not what
your Monger tells you is most important. We are going to name
your values because your values will help guide you to what
comes next.

As Brené Brown says, "There are no guarantees in the arena.
We will struggle. We will even fail. There will be darkness. But
if we are clear about the values that guide us in our efforts to
show up and be seen, we will always be able to find the light."[1]

When you can get honest with yourself and name your values, they will become the new standards of how you live your
life. No longer will you be driven by external standards set by
the Monger; now you will have internal guides to chart your
course.

Here are how values play out in Samantha's life.

When her Monger is in charge: Samantha is the Activities Chair for her local women's group. They are having their yearly kickoff meeting on Friday and she is a mess. Her Monger keeps telling her how everything must be *perfect*. She has been running around all week gathering supplies, answering emails, and responding to texts. She can't sleep because she keeps running her to-do list through her head and her Monger is constantly telling her everything she missed and how the whole thing is a complete failure. Samantha loves this group and is so excited for the kickoff event *and* she is driving herself crazy listening to her Monger chime on and on about how it is not going to go well.

When her Biggest Fan reminds her of her values: Samantha is the Activities Chair for her local women's group. They are having their yearly kickoff meeting on Friday and she is a mess. Her Monger keeps telling her how everything must be *perfect*. She has been running around all week gathering supplies, answering emails, and responding to texts. Finally, Samantha implements A.S.K. When she gets to K. Kindly pull back to see the big picture, her Biggest Fan says, "Okay, what is most important here?"

Samantha remembers her values and says to herself, Relationships, humor, and emotional health are in my top five, and with my Monger running the show none of those are being met."

Throughout the week, when Samantha hears her Monger she runs through A.S.K. and reminds herself that it isn't about perfection; it is about con-

WHAT'S MOST IMPORTANT TO YOU? | 131

necting with the women, laughing, and feeling grounded and centered no matter what comes up.

By focusing on her values, Samantha is able to bring herself back to what really matters here. When we don't have values as a guide, it is easy to get in a tit-for-tat argument with our Monger (which we will always lose). Our Monger's top value is perfection, and if we are not aware of our own values, perfection will always win out.

So when your Monger starts running the show, you can A.S.K. to hear from your Biggest Fan and use your values to help see the bigger picture. Knowing your values helps with the final step of A.S.K., Kindly pull back to see the big picture, and helps you know what is most important.

WHAT ARE VALUES?

So, what are values? As defined by the *Merriam-Webster.com Dictionary*, a value is "something (such as a principle or quality) intrinsically valuable or desirable."[2]

Values are the foundation of your life. Values are the guiding principles on which everything else builds. Values help you answer the question, What's most important here? The values you choose and the definitions you give them are unique to you. Someone may share similar values to yours, but their definitions might be different.

Too often we aren't living by our values. We find ourselves caught up in the messages of our Monger and we are doing what we think we should do or what so-and-so is doing. When we are living a life based on someone else's values, we end up feeling numb, disengaged, and uninspired by our life.

In contrast, your Biggest Fan encourages you to live true to your values. Your values provide a simple, easy way to see the big picture and determine what is most important to you so you can take the next steps.

When I work with clients on values, I encourage them to pick their top five values. You will get a chance to do this later in the chapter. These top five values serve as the foundation to make new decisions in our lives so we can live a life more engaged and inspired.

Your values are expressed in the decisions you make and the activities you choose. Imagine someone was silently observing your life:

- What would they see you valuing the most?
- Would they be able to tell what you valued most by looking at how you spend your time and with whom you spend it?

If you are living your life from your values, then the decisions you make and the commitments you engage in will support one of your top five values. Let's say family is one of your top five values; then your life decisions will revolve around supporting and engaging with your family. You won't want to engage in activities or spend time with people who take you away from your family for a long period. Your family is consistently a priority.

If you value social change, you make everyday choices that inspire social change through the clothes you wear, the websites you visit, and the products you use. You may want to work in a job or support causes that encourage social change and work towards the social change you want to see.

If you value creativity, then you probably engage in activities that feed your artistic side, whether it is through drawing, painting, developing ideas, or writing. Expressing your creative side through either paid or unpaid activities will be a focus of your life.

Only you can define what a value means for you. For example, many people value financial security. For one person that could mean having just enough money to pay all the bills, while for another person that could mean paying all the bills and having money left over to take as many vacations as they want.

OLD VALUES/OTHER PEOPLE'S VALUES

Growing up you learned values from teachers, parents, clergy, and friends. Now as an adult you are entitled to your own values. Our Biggest Fan helps us get clear on and live out our values.

Our Monger loves to remind us of other people's values. She loves to hold on to old values that belonged to our parents that might not be our values today. For example, maybe your parents found it important to go to church and religion was one of their values, but you value family, and Sunday mornings are the only time your immediate family has time to hang out, catch up, and bond so you don't want to spend that time at church. *That is okay.* Remember, values and guilt don't go together. Values aren't shoulds. They are intentions that resonate with you and answer the question, What is most important here? You need to let go of the guilt of not sharing someone else's values.

For example, your father values loyalty, so he worked at the same employer for 30+ years and encouraged you to do the same. However, maybe you value learning and you have learned all you can from your current employer. Even though you have only been there for five years, you want to find another employer where you can continue to learn and grow. Recognizing this difference and knowing that you can make different choices and have different values is key.

Maybe you have outgrown a value. I remember in my 20s I really valued social acceptance and would head out every weekend with my friends to see the latest movie just so I could say I had been there and done that. Today? I spend Friday nights quietly with my nearest and dearest or close friends, and the thought of facing the throngs of people to see the latest movie makes my skin crawl! It was great for my 20s, but now that I am almost 45, I value relationships more than I value social acceptance and I would rather pass. Imagine if I listened to my Monger who told me I *should* value social acceptance—I would be stressed out every Friday night.

Your top five values reflect *you,* not what you have been told to do or have been expected to do.

CONFLICTING VALUES

Our top five values may not be similar to each other and might be in direct conflict with each other. Rarely do all your values exist without a little conflict with each other. Here is where your Monger will be quick to come in and tell you how wrong you are and how you can't live a life with values that aren't similar. But your Biggest Fan is there to remind you that you can pull back and look at the big picture. You can include all your values; you just need to be more creative, not critical.

For example, maybe you value risk taking but you also value logic so you are an auditor who bungee jumps. Or you value financial security and creativity so you might be working a variety of jobs to fulfill both your creative outlet and your need for a secure future. You might work as a freelance writer to feed your creative side and have a job as a nurse to pay the bills. Or you value independence but you also value socializing so you need to be conscious and intentional about making sure you build quality relationships with others while also balancing your need for freedom, individuality, or autonomy.

Bottom line: conflicting values are not a lost cause. Don't let your Monger win on this one. Your Biggest Fan will lovingly lead the way.

SELECT YOUR TOP FIVE VALUES

On the following page is a chart for you to use in selecting your top five values. Use these instructions:

- X out the ones that are obviously *not* values for you.
- Draw a box around those that are a maybe.
- Draw a circle around the yes values.
- Narrow down the list until there are only your top five values.
- You can add or combine as many values that you feel have a similar definition.

Helpful hints for this process:

- Picking your top five values is supposed to be challenging so make sure you give yourself some time. You don't have to do it all in one sitting.
- As you do this exercise, be on the lookout for your Monger. She will try to derail you and bring you down. Take a minute to slow down and get into your body so you can channel your Biggest Fan before you start.
- This list is a starting point; feel free to add other values or combine values if you wish.
- Your top 2–3 values will probably pop out at you.
- You probably have lots of these words as values; the assignment is just to pick your top five. Just because it isn't on the top five list doesn't mean it isn't a value. Don't get caught up in the idea that you aren't kind because compassion isn't in your top five values. You can be kind and it just isn't a top value for you (and that's okay).

LIST OF VALUES

Achievement	Advancement	Adventure
Affection	Altruism	Appearance
Approval	Authority	Autonomy
Beauty	Challenge	Charity
Community	Compassion	Creativity
Dependability	Environment	Empathy
Expertise	Fame	Family
Financial Security	Freedom	Generosity
Health (emotional)	Health (physical)	Home
Honesty	Humility	Humor
Independence	Integrity	Intelligence
Learning	Leisure	Logic
Love	Loyalty	Meaning
Openness	Patriotism	Peace
Perseverance	Personal Growth	Popularity
Power	Privacy	Recognition
Relationships	Religion	Reputation
Risk Taking	Security	Simplicity
Social Acceptance	Socializing	Solitude
Spiritual Development	Status	Trustworthy
Thrift	Winning	Wisdom

To print visit: http://live-happier.com/the-happier-approach-giveaways/

Now that you know your top five values, we are going to look at them a little deeper.

For each value, answer the following questions:

1. **What is your definition of the value?** Take some time to think about how you would define the value— not what the dictionary says or what your friends would say, but how *you* define the value. This question brings more clarity to how each value is going to show up in your life.

2. **What activities do you engage in that express this value?** If someone all-knowing were to observe your life (like a fly on the wall) how would she/he see this value played out? I call this the Come-to-Jesus Question. It is a litmus test of whether this is really your value. If you don't have activities that you engage in that reflect this value, the next question to ask is, Is this really a value of mine or is it a value I think I *should* have?

   If the answer is no, it is not a value of yours, go back to the list and select a value that is in your top five.

   If the answer is yes, and you just don't have any activities that support that value currently, move on to question 3.

3. **What activities do you need to add or delete to better express this value?** What changes do you need to make to showcase this value in your life?

I encourage you to visit this exercise repeatedly, because your values might change over time. Reminding yourself of your values and their definitions is important. The answers to these questions show you what activities are most important to you. When your Monger starts chatting about what you *should*

138 | THE HAPPIER APPROACH

be doing, you can return to your values list and ask, Does this activity fit my values? If it does, you can pursue that activity with the kindness of your Biggest Fan. If it doesn't, you can let that activity go and choose one that is more in line with your values.

CONCLUSION

Bottom line, we are happier when we live by *our* values, not what our Monger tells us we *should be* living by. After years of listening to your Monger telling you what you *should* be doing, listening to your own values will be challenging because your Monger's message has become your default. Initially, you will need to remind yourself of your values as often as possible. Some of my clients have written their values down and framed them to display in their office. You can post them in your home, put them on your phone, and share them with your family. Accountability is helpful, so encourage your family to lovingly remind you of your values when they notice you are spinning out from a Monger attack.

Knowing your values is the next level in being able to see the big picture. Our values provide the framework for our lives. Based on that framework we can decide what steps to take next. Knowing and living your values can quickly quiet a Monger attack.

CHAPTER TEN

Change Is Possible—It Just Isn't Easy

" All change is incremental.
ll change is incremental.
ll change is incremental," my counseling instructor said in a booming voice. Every time we talked about helping our clients make change, he would bellow this phrase at top volume to remind us that change takes time and it isn't easy. It stuck with me and is one reason I wanted to include a chapter on change.

When you are trying to change a default pattern in your life, quieting the Monger is challenging. Changing your motivation from shame and belittling to kindness and wisdom is challenging. It is easy to read this book; it is not so easy to implement the strategies discussed. This chapter offers some helpful hints on what to expect as you make these changes and what to do when you hit the inevitable challenges. I invite you to return to this chapter when you get snagged and feel discouraged.

THE PROCESS OF CHANGE

Visualize a spiral staircase that serves as a continuum. At the bottom is Mongerville, where you allow your Monger to boss you around and belittle you. At the top is the Land of the Biggest Fan, where you are only listening to your Biggest Fan and she is kind and full of wisdom.

The spiral staircase is long and winding and there are many stops along the way. As you make change you move up the staircase. Slowly, slowly, slowly you progress up the staircase, moving closer to the Land of the Biggest Fan. The truth is, some days you might move up and some days you might move down. That is okay. Change is a *process*. To move up the staircase closer to the Land of the Biggest Fan, you need to focus on two actions: building non-judgmental awareness of the Monger and using A.S.K. to hear from your Biggest Fan.

Building Non-Judgmental Awareness of the Monger

You can't quiet the voice of the Monger until you notice how often it is chatting at you. Notice the behaviors you engage in that bring her out to play. Get to know when she chats, what she chats about, and how you feel when she chats.

Notice I said *non-judgmental* awareness. As you build awareness of your Monger, the temptation is to judge yourself for judging yourself (yet another irony!), but the truth is that only through acceptance and awareness can change occur.

As Carl Rogers said in *On Becoming a Person,* "The curious paradox is that when I accept myself just as I am, then I can change."[1]

Understanding the Monger's patterns and themes will allow you to recognize her faster so she doesn't talk on and on unchecked. When you live in Mongerville, starting to build awareness is a humbling process. You will be *shocked* how often she pops up and how mean she is.

Use A.S.K. to Hear from Your Biggest Fan

Here is where the continuum staircase analogy comes into play. At the beginning of your work when you are at the Mongerville portion of the staircase, it will take you a little while to notice the Monger. Because your Monger is so comfortable and familiar, there will be a time gap between when your Monger starts chatting and when you notice her chatting.

Noticing your Monger is challenging, even when you have been practicing this stuff for years. You might be getting attacked by your Monger for days before you notice her. Or you might have the awareness the same day that when you ate the whole pan of brownies you were trying to numb out your Monger. That's okay. Remember the mantra, "All change is incremental."

The key to change is whenever you notice your Monger take action, to A.S.K. to hear from your Biggest Fan. Gradually over time you will move up the spiral staircase and you will keep shortening the gap between awareness and action.

Change takes time and yes, the process can be frustrating, especially for those of us who want to do it right and be perfect. Build awareness of your Monger. Take action and shorten that gap. Stick with it and it will pay off.

SOME STRAIGHT TALK

The goal is to spend more time in the Land of the Biggest Fan, but the truth is you will always be moving up and down this staircase. It isn't like you arrive in the Land of the Biggest Fan and stay there forever.

Be kind to yourself when you find yourself being attacked by your Monger and remember this is a process. The victory comes when we can recognize our Monger and quiet her with the Biggest Fan.

Following are some ideas and concepts that snag us as we move up this spiral staircase of change.

INSTANT GRATIFICATION

We love the idea of change and we all know *how* to make change.

Want to lose weight? Eat less.

Want to build strong abs? Do sit-ups.

Want to quiet your nasty internal voice? Be kind to yourself.

So we know the steps we could be taking. The problem is it is hard to consistently show up day after day and make small changes without an immediate payoff. In a society where we are inundated with advertisements and commercials promising "lose 20 pounds in two weeks" or "earn six figures in six months," it is easy to get discouraged when the payoff isn't instant. We live in a world of instant gratification.

The idea that we have to *do* the work and it will be hard and frustrating and we *will* fail (gasp!) sucks. I want you to hear me: it is 100 percent normal to get frustrated with yourself. The key is picking yourself back up off the floor and trying again. Continue working even when you fail.

One of the most important parts of changing a behavior is what to do when you inevitably fail. It is how to pick yourself up when you notice you fell off the wagon. It is all about building resilience.

Our Monger trained us that resilience is scary and unknown, because to practice resilience we have to practice showing up and making a mistake.

Our Monger is all about instant gratification (i.e., making one simple change and having a huge payoff that sticks). Not surprisingly, this desire for instant gratification leads to disappointment, and that leads to a battle between our Monger and our BFF. Too often we stop the process of change before we even start because it feels so uncomfortable.

Here's how Samantha struggles with instant gratification:

Samantha wants to get in better shape. After much debate, she decides she will hop on the treadmill every day for 30 minutes. She reasons that she used to run in college so it should be easy to pick back up. The first day she runs for 20 minutes. It was exhausting and she felt like she was going to die, but she survived and feels good about her workout. The next day her alarm goes off and she thinks to herself, No way. As she rolls over to turn off her alarm she feels a sharp pain in her legs. "Ouch!" she cries out. She hasn't felt this sore since college.

"You are so out of shape; you can't even run 20 minutes without being unable to move. That is pathetic," her Monger chimes in.

"Roll over and go back to bed. Twenty minutes was a lot! Being sore sucks! You need to rest," her BFF counters.

Throughout the day, Samantha's Monger and BFF go back and forth a few times until finally her BFF wins and Samantha decides it is too hard to get back into shape. The BFF's and Monger's constant chatter combined with sore muscles and no instant gratification convinces Samantha to stop. Thus ends Samantha's attempt to get in better shape.

But the next day Samantha wakes up and remembers that she is trying to listen to her Biggest Fan more. She reminds herself to not get stuck in instant gratification and practice A.S.K.

Here is what her Biggest Fan might say. "Wow, this is so painful. Being sore hurts and it is such a blow. Stop and breathe. I mean you knew you were out of shape but you didn't think you were *this* out of shape. Take today off and rest and regroup. But *no way* is this the end of your quest to be in better shape. This was just the wakeup call that you needed to start slower. Maybe just walk for 15 minutes every other day or do a walk/run combo for 15 minutes. This is all one big experiment with the end goal of getting in better shape, not another reason to beat yourself up."

Samantha's Biggest Fan helped her break down the steps into smaller, more manageable pieces.

So often clients come into my office beating themselves up for "failing again," when in reality they may have tried to make too big of a change in too short of a time. We want to run before we can walk and we want to walk before we crawl. As Bill Murray's character in *What about Bob?* says, "Baby steps, all I have to do is take one step at a time and I can do anything!"[2]

To make real change we must remember that we are preprogrammed for instant gratification. Give yourself permission to take small, manageable steps. Expect and plan for the inevitable frustration and keep moving forward. Most importantly, pick yourself up again when it doesn't work. When you hit a snag, channel your Biggest Fan and see if you can find smaller steps.

BEATING YOURSELF UP WON'T HELP

Let's check in with Samantha as she struggles with a problem we all have, using her phone too much.

Samantha decides she is too addicted to her phone, so she is only going to use it for phone calls and texts. No more Facebook, Pinterest, Instagram, or Candy Crush. She is *done* and she is turning her phone off to everything except calls and texts. As she moves through the day she misses randomly checking her phone but for the most part it goes okay. By day 3, however, she is really jonesing for her phone. She missed the picture of her cousin's new baby and she loves looking at Pinterest for new recipes.

As she is waiting at the doctor's office, her BFF chimes in, "Come on, you deserve to look at your phone. We are just sitting here with nothing to do; it's not like it is going to hurt anything."

"You are so weak. Come on. You can't even keep a commitment to yourself about one little thing. You really are addicted," says her Monger.

"A few minutes won't hurt. I mean the spirit of this whole thing was to not use your phone in front of the kids, and they aren't here. Go ahead just check Facebook."

Her BFF wins. She pulls out her phone and settles in to kill a few minutes checking Facebook and playing Candy Crush.

As she is driving home from the doctor's appointment, she hears her Monger, "Wow, you really can't even go without your phone for three days. You might as well give up this charade and admit you are a failure. Just like last time."

And that is it. She gives up her desire to change her phone use. She just goes back to using it all the time and admits to herself that she is a weak, addicted fool who can't say no to her phone.

Truth is we fail. We aren't always successful. When we fail, the tendency is for our Monger to come out and shame us. But beating ourselves up for the fact that we aren't successful isn't the answer. Beating ourselves up will not make us want to try again.

Think about it. If your son does poorly on a math test and you say to him, "You are so stupid! How could you be *this* bad at math. I mean seriously you are terrible. Head to your room and figure it out because you have to get this grade up!" do you think he would be motivated to run to his room and start figuring out math? (Probably not!)

But if you said to your son, "Oh, sweetheart, that just feels terrible to fail a math test. Let's review the test and see where you succeeded and where you struggled. Maybe we need to find a tutor or figure out a way to help you study better. You can do this math stuff. We just have to figure out how to help you learn it best!"

When you beat yourself up you aren't going to want to try again and are more likely to quit. Samantha probably won't try again with her phone for a while. The beatdown she gave herself was pretty harsh and she probably won't have the energy to do it differently for a period of time. But if she gave herself caring encouragement and empathy and recognized that failure is part of the process, she might have made real progress to overcome her phone addiction.

Our tendency is to want to make big sweeping changes, like going to the extreme of *only* using your phone for calls/texts. And if we can't make that change perfectly the first time we try, we completely give up on the change.

In reality, there are lots of baby steps we could take. When we fail, it is important to look at what caused us to fail so we can make the necessary changes. When we fail, we need to A.S.K.

Here's what Samantha's Biggest Fan had to say:

> "Okay, let's be real, going from using your phone 24/7 to *never* using it might be a bit of a stretch. That is *really* hard, my love!! I get it, failure sucks, but you didn't totally ruin it and you aren't a loser because you used it one time at the doctor's office. Let's take a pause; maybe we need to rethink this and make some easier rules to follow. The phone isn't 100 percent evil. It helps you decom-

press and stay connected. Your goal is to not get lost in your phone because you value family.

"So why don't you create more options:

1. What if we put a time limit so you can do social media/play games for one hour a day. I am sure there is an app to monitor that.

2. You don't want to use it around your kids, so what if you can only use it at certain times, like waiting at the doctor's office or when you aren't with the kids?"

See how that worked? Samantha's Biggest Fan was not only kind but curious and was able to provide some new strategies for making the change.

SPIRALING UP

One thing with change that rarely gets mentioned is a concept I call Spiraling Up. As you travel up the spiral staircase from Mongerville to the Land of the Biggest Fan, you visit the same place on the spiral but one level up.

Frequently I have clients who come into my office and say, "I thought I fixed this; why am I going through it again?" And I will reply, "You did fix this, but now you are learning how to do it at another level."

Something we tend to forget about life lessons is that we keep learning more and more until we have them mastered. We might come back to the lesson and it might feel like we are re-learning the same lesson, but really, we are experiencing it at a new level with a new insight, a new situation, a new challenge. And then when we have that mastered, we will spiral up to another place.

You might have learned how to deal with your Monger at home, but it is a little more challenging at work, where you find your Monger runs the show. So you learn a similar lesson about your Monger but now it is at work. You will have leveled up into a more difficult area but still the lesson will seem familiar.

When you think about life lessons as Spiraling Up, it gives a new perspective. While we do repeat lessons, we don't unlearn all we have implemented before. We repeat the lesson one step up with new perspective, new challenges, and new information that we didn't have the last time the lesson came into our lives. So the next time you have a sense of déjà vu when it comes to a life lesson, don't beat yourself up. Remind yourself that you aren't failing, you are just Spiraling Up.

THE DO-OVER

Remember when you would play a game as a child and something would go horribly wrong (you whiffed the ball, missed the goal, or completely tanked the basket), and someone would scream "do-over"? It simply meant try again. No harm, no foul; you get a free pass to try it all again. It is one of my favorite things to cry out whenever we play darts (which I *love* playing and am terrible at). Frequently I will completely miss the board, the dart will fall to the ground, and I'll say "do-over!" Embracing the do-over in darts has allowed me to enjoy the game *and* improve my level of play.

Here are some great examples of do-overs:

- You realize mid-sentence that the words coming out of your mouth are not phrased the way you want them to be and the conversation is not going well. You pause and ask, "Can we start over?"
- In the middle of an argument you realize it has taken a very bad turn. You can simply pause and say, "Let's pause and regroup here."
- You end a conversation with a friend and worry that there might have been a misunderstanding, so you

simply call them and say, "Can we do that conversation over?"

- After walking away from a business meeting, you realize you might have joked at the wrong moment at a co-worker's expense, so you go to their office and say, "I want to apologize for making a bad joke..."

As adults, we don't grant ourselves a lot of do-overs. However, do-overs are a necessity in the practice of making change. Anytime we are learning something new, practicing something different, or trying to improve ourselves, we need room to make mistakes and correct them with compassion and empathy—thus the do-over. Our Monger doesn't embrace the do-over. She would rather have you stay stuck in self-blame. So whenever you are spinning out on a mistake, ask yourself, Is there room for a do-over?

The do-over is going to be one of the keys to making changes with your Monger. Giving yourself permission to try again and do it differently will make a big difference in your life.

CONCLUSION

The title of this chapter says it all: change is possible, it just isn't easy. So be kind to yourself. Give yourself a lot of grace. Changing these patterns is challenging and requires resiliency. One step at a time you can move up the spiral staircase away from Mongerville and into the Land of the Biggest Fan. I know it.

CHAPTER ELEVEN

Q&A

We made it. I hope this book has given you not only a different way of thinking about the voices in your head but also strategies and inspiration for channeling your Biggest Fan.

Your Monger has been running the show for quite some time, so of course there is going to be some confusion as to what life would look like without the consistent shame and drama that the Monger brought in.

There is something oddly comforting about our Monger. As in that analogy of the old sweater I used before, it is okay that you have some confusion on how to let her go.

I have gathered some common Q&As I have heard over the years as I have worked with clients on the concepts discussed in this book. Please revisit this chapter whenever you feel confused or lost and need some extra guidance.

HOW WILL I KNOW MY BIGGEST FAN IS TALKING?

It is hard at first. The voice of the Biggest Fan is quiet after years of being ignored. Plus, when you have lived your life shaming/belittling yourself into submission, the idea of being kind and trusting yourself can be a hard pill to swallow. So initially, her voice is quiet and her vocabulary is small.

Here's a recent example from my life.

Writing this book frequently brought up my Monger. There is a lot of risk of being rejected, so holding my feet to the fire and sitting down at the computer has been a challenge.

When I was on day 3 of no writing and I had spent yet another day surfing the internet and comparing myself to all the other amazing authors out there, I looked up from my computer and saw it was 3 pm. "Well, you are never going to finish this book. Who do you think you are? You can never complete anything. Another great idea bites the dust," my Monger grumbled.

"Take the rest of the day off; clearly you aren't going to get anything done. Let's go downstairs and watch *Real Housewives*. I think there is ice cream in the fridge," cheered my BFF.

"No! You should stick to it. You *have* to write. You promised yourself you would finish this and you *have* to keep writing. You are always quitting," my Monger insisted.

I sighed and used A.S.K. to hear from my Biggest Fan. "I get this. It is scary to be so vulnerable and put your thoughts out there on paper. Stand up and stretch. What if you tried to write for 10 minutes and that is it?" my Biggest Fan suggested. "If it doesn't work you will take a break."

10 minutes pass, and I find myself back on the internet. Another hour passes with more time spent surfing the internet.

"Okay, girl, either write or do something else— sitting here surfing the internet is *not* helping. You have to be in the headspace to write and clearly you aren't, so sitting here is silly. Let's go down-stairs and do something that feeds you. Maybe that is reading a book or watching *Real Housewives*. But sitting here isn't cutting it."

Is that my Biggest Fan or my BFF talking!?

I take a deep breath and get into my body and I admit to myself I am feeling tired and unmotivated. Maybe today isn't the day to write. Writers block is real. The more I sit here and force my writing, the less I will enjoy writing in the future. So I will take the rest of the day off, but first I will make a plan for the rest of the week. Maybe sitting at home isn't the place. Maybe I need to shut off the internet and maybe I need to stick to a number of words per day goal. I make a plan for the rest of the week: I will head to the library to write and meet a minimum word count each day.

So, the answer is, it isn't cut and dry.

As a simple reminder:

- Your Monger shames and belittles you.
- Your BFF shames and belittles other people in defense of you and has the amazing talent of always being able to justify any behavior.
- Your Biggest Fan always has your back, acknowledges your feelings, can see options, is wise about the struggle, and uses your values as guiding principles.

Here are a few sample scenarios with your Monger, BFF, and Biggest Fan. As you read through these, pay attention to the subtle differences between the BFF's voice and the Biggest Fan's voice. Use these as a reference point for when you are feeling confused and unsure of whose voice you are hearing.

Scenario: Your staff is behind on their goals for the month.

Monger: You are a terrible leader. If you were better at your job this wouldn't be happening. If only you could actually motivate them, loser.

BFF: You are doing a great job; they are just lazy. I mean you can only work with what you have. It's not your fault they can't get it together.

Biggest Fan: *(A. Acknowledge what you are feeling)* Ugh! This is so disappointing. You try so hard and I know you *really* want your team to succeed. *(S. Slow down and get into your body)* Stretch your neck and take some deep breaths. *(K. Kindly pull back to see the big picture)* You have implemented all the strategies you can think of and they still can't hit the goals. Maybe we need to re-think these goals. Or meet with each of them and figure out what is going on so you can find some different strategies. You aren't a bad leader; you just don't have the strategies yet to hit these marks.

Scenario: You binge watch *Orange Is the New Black* rather than working in the yard like you had planned.

Monger: You are such a loser. On top of being lazy, you can't keep your word. You said you were going to do yard work. You already have the worst-looking yard in the neighborhood and now you wasted yet another day doing nothing.

BFF: You work so hard during the week. You *deserve* to do nothing. Screw the neighbors—they don't have lives anyway. All they do is take care of their yards. You have a life and you know that there is more to the world than just keeping a pristine yard. Enjoy your day of nothing.

Biggest Fan: (*A. Acknowledge what you are feeling*) It is okay to be conflicted. On one hand, you must have needed a day of nothing *and* you did say you would take care of the yard. (*S. Slow down and get into your body*) Stand up and stretch, take some deep breaths. (*K. Kindly pull back to see the big picture*) The truth is, you love this show *and* being able to binge watch is a special treat. Soak it up and enjoy! And the lawn does need to be mowed. You love driving past the house and seeing the yard look nice, so maybe tomorrow after lunch you can just do some quick cleanup.

Scenario: There is a celebration in the office and everyone is eating pizza and cake for lunch.

Monger: You are a fat ass. You *say* you are committed to healthy eating, but at the first sign of pizza you inhale it all. You are *never* going to lose weight.

BFF: It's a special occasion. You *should* be celebrating. I mean how often does your co-worker turn 40. You don't want to look uptight and rigid. Dive in, enjoy! You totally deserve this; you have been good for the past three days.

Biggest Fan: (*A. Acknowledge what you are feeling*) Yum. Pizza and cake! You love pizza and cake! And you have been trying to honor your value of physical health. You want to fit in and eat like everyone else *and* eat healthy. (*S. Slow down and get into your body*) Take a pause, feel your feet on the ground, and take some deep breaths. (*K. Kindly pull back to see the big picture*) Enjoy—and remember you are practicing the skill of noticing when you are full. So eat slowly, pay attention, and stop when you get full. When you eat too much, you feel tired and sluggish the rest of the day. Enjoy *and* be mindful.

Scenario: You get called out at work for missing a deadline.

Monger: You are totally going to get fired. How could you miss the deadline? You are so stupid and lazy.

BFF: What do they think you are, a machine? I mean they demand way too much from you. How can they expect you to get *all* of this done? They are crazy! They have no grounds for firing you because their expectations are insane! I mean what more do they expect from you?

Biggest Fan: (*A. Acknowledge what you are feeling*) Wow, that sucks. You hate disappointing people and being called out at the staff meeting. Ouch. That hurts. Ugh. (*S. Slow down and get into your body*) Take a minute to give yourself some regroup time. Stretch your hands over your head and breathe. (*K. Kindly pull back to see the big picture*) Here's the thing. Last week was crazy. There was so much going on and this just slipped through the cracks. It wasn't like you weren't working. You were just working on a different priority. Why don't you chat with your boss and the team to clear the air and make sure it doesn't happen again.

SO, HAVE YOU GOTTEN RID OF YOUR MONGER?

The most frequent question people ask me is, "So, have you gotten rid of your Monger?" And my answer is always no, but she no longer controls my every move. In practicing these concepts your Monger won't have a hold on your life anymore *and* she won't go away permanently. She will still be there, but her voice will be less loud. She won't stay around as long and your Biggest Fan will jump in to help out much more often.

There is no happier finish line in life. Happiness is not static; it is ever flowing. There will be times in your life when you are feeling happier than other times. But as long as you are perpetually chasing happiness, it will elude you. The irony is that the ever-elusive peace comes from letting go of the reins, not holding on to them tighter.

What I love about embracing the voice of our Biggest Fan is that she has the capacity to live in the real world, in all its messiness. She can teach us how to be scrambling at work to meet a deadline and enjoy a laugh with a co-worker. Or be in the middle of a sleepless night with your baby—tired, worn out, and ready to cry—and also be overwhelmed with the joy of being a mother. She can support you in crying at the loss of your father while being in awe of the gold of the sunset.

So no, I haven't gotten rid of my Monger, but the lens through which I view my life is more often the Biggest Fan's. I am not ashamed of my Monger, just aware of her. Gone are the days when all I saw was how far I had to go. Now I can see how far I have come and offer myself grace in the rest of the journey.

I stopped drinking the Monger Kool-Aid that all would be perfect and started living the authentic messy life that is 100 percent uniquely mine.

AFTER READING THE BOOK, I STILL THINK I NEED SOME SHAME TO GET STUFF DONE. HOW DO I TRUST THAT I CAN BE SUCCESSFUL WITHOUT THE SHAME?

I hear you. You believe that without shame you will be a lazy binge-watching, ice cream–eating loser. Shame is what makes you productive and accomplished. I get it. I have been there, as have many of my clients.

And you are *wrong*.

You are going just to have to trust me on this one. I know because I believed that too. I spent way too many years believing that. And now on the other side, when I hear more from my Biggest Fan than I do my Monger, I can say I accomplish *far* more. I would never have written this book without my Biggest Fan because the shame and belittling the Monger threw at me would have been paralyzing.

I challenge you to try it for 30 days. When you hear your Monger, A.S.K. to hear from your Biggest Fan:

Acknowledge what you are feeling.

Slow down and get into your body.

Kindly pull back to see the big picture.

Even if you love to procrastinate and up until now feel like your Monger is the only reason you get anything done, you are wrong. Trusting your Biggest Fan will make sure you get stuff done. Maybe not on the timeline you think you *should* get it done, but you will accomplish stuff. Your motivation will be different. Rather than cleaning your house because you *should* or because you are worried about what the neighbors think, you will clean your house because you decide what areas of your house matter to you. You will decide if you enjoy a clean bathroom or kitchen. You will decide what's more important, vacuuming or clutter.

And when you trust yourself to make those decisions, you *will* check things off your to-do list. Without all the outside pressure to do it right and/or perfectly, you will complete the tasks on your timeline based on your priorities.

Samantha can show you what I mean.

> Samantha takes a big sigh and looks around her. The house is empty; her sons and husband went fishing. She *should* do some cleaning, but it is the last thing she wants to do.

"This place is a pit. What if the neighbors popped over? You are such a slacker. Get off your butt and start cleaning. It is going to take you all afternoon to get this stuff done," her Monger says.

Her BFF chimes in, "It's fine; no one cares what the house looks like. Enjoy your day of quiet. The house looks fine."

Samantha thinks to herself, Okay, I am not dealing with you two today. I need to channel my Biggest Fan. What does she have to say about this one?

"First off, I get it that you are feeling overwhelmed, tired of trying to live up to these crazy expectations. Slow down; let's take a deep breath and touch your toes. I mean who cares if the house looks messy if the neighbors pop over. I think it shows that you actually live here."

But her Monger isn't done, "Such a typical excuse, the lived-in excuse. So you want to live in a pigsty because you are too lazy to clean up?"

"You are not too lazy to clean, you just don't value a spotless house. You value living your life and making sure you are baseline cleanly. The clutter drives you crazy and you want to do the occasional vacuum. These standards you have been holding yourself to are way too high, and for whom? Who is benefitting from them? How often do the neighbors 'pop in' for no reason?" says her Biggest Fan.

Samantha decided to clean her house on *her* terms, not on some unachievable scale set by her Monger. She picks up the clutter that fills the family room and vacuums. Then she decides to grab her new book and enjoy the peaceful backyard all by herself.

So try it: for the next 30 days experiment with your Biggest Fan and see if you become less or more accomplished.

DO I HAVE TO GET INTO MY BODY?
I JUST DON'T GET HOW THAT HELPS.

This is by far the one area I get the most pushback on. And trust me, it is the one area I had the most pushback from myself on. It is so hard to get into your body because it is the last thing you want to do.

And *yes*, it is necessary! If there was a way to do this without getting into your body, I would have figured it out. I tried and tried. The reasons we are so resistant to getting into our bodies are also the reasons it is so important.

We are so resistant to getting into our bodies partially because as women we are at war with our bodies—that idea of never being skinny enough, fit enough, or healthy enough. Getting into our body starts to bridge the gap. It helps us start to make peace and come to acceptance with who we are and the shape of the vessel that allows us to move through the world.

When we get into our bodies it forces us to slow down, and slowing down allows us to feel, and we don't want to feel. However, facing our feelings is what gives our Biggest Fan so much power! When we aren't running scared from how we feel we don't get as caught up in anxiety and stress.

So yes, you *have to* get into your body. The Mindfulness Hacks discussed in Chapter 7 make that as easy as possible. It doesn't have to be some drawn-out process of 20 minutes of meditation or 10 minutes of yoga. It can be as simple as going barefoot, stretching up to the sky, touching your toes, or taking three deep breaths. The more you do it the less painful it is. I promise.

I KEEP GETTING STUCK. I AM TRYING TO BUILD AWARENESS OF MY MONGER, BUT AS YOU SAY SHE IS WILY. IT SEEMS LIKE SHE IS ALWAYS WINNING. WILL SHE EVER BE QUIET?

The Monger is definitely wily. No doubt about it! She has become so woven into our lives we have a hard time separating her out. So first off, give yourself a break. Remember baby steps, baby steps, baby steps (Chapter 10). Maybe you start with one myth (Chapter 2) and try to pay attention to that for two weeks, or pick one situation your Monger is always chiming on about and focus on that. Every time you hear your Monger chat about that myth/situation, practice A.S.K. to hear from your Biggest Fan.

Sometimes we need an outside perspective to help us hear/see our Monger. Ask someone you love and trust—your spouse, your best friend, a sibling—to lovingly remind you when you are engaging in one of your myths or you are being exceptionally harsh on yourself. This can be hard, so prepare yourself for lots of do-overs.

Having that outside help can make the process easier. I made a lot more progress when my husband lovingly mirrored how often I was trying to "do it right." The more he pointed it out to me the easier it was for me to see the habit, and the more frequently I could access my Biggest Fan.

Spend more time on accessing your Biggest Fan rather than listening for your Monger. Randomly throughout the day, do something physical, get into your body, and tap into your feelings.

For so many years our Monger has convinced us she knows better, so initially working with our Biggest Fan is going to take some trust. Being open to the idea that kindness can be motivating and shaming ourselves makes us more stressed and miserable is key.

Pretend that your whole life you were told spinach was bad for you. Your mom hated spinach and didn't want it in the house, so she told you that spinach was bad for you and never bothered to tell you different. And then suddenly in your 20s you hear spinach is good for you and you are like "What!?!" you can't believe it. You do a lot of research and everything you read says spinach is healthy. But when you first start eating spinach it feels like you are going to die because your brain is telling you this is bad for you, even though you have done all the research and you know it might be different. But you have to go against your brain and trust it is good.

That is a tongue-and-cheek example, but it illustrates the point that our Biggest Fan is good for us but we don't trust her at first. Our Monger tends to be the first responder. She is always the loudest and quickest. One of my favorite mantras has become "First thought wrong." When I hear my Monger chatting at me I will say to myself, Okay, first thought wrong! Then I will A.S.K. to hear from my Biggest Fan.

Finally, go easy on yourself. You have spent your life being an overachiever so your tendency is to overachieve on quieting your Monger as well. Remember you are a *work in process*. The process just takes time.

THIS IS CRAZY TO SAY, BUT SOMETIMES I MISS MY MONGER. IS THAT NORMAL?

Ha! I totally understand that one. It isn't crazy; it is totally understandable. We have had a relationship with this voice for most of our lives, so of course you are going to miss it. Not to mention that she would bring a lot of drama and distraction into your life. As much as you hated that, it also served as a way to break out of your normal hum-drum everyday life.

I have found that a lot of people (myself included) are surprised how much they miss their Monger. I even felt lonely and frustrated without her. When you stop listening to her all the time, you realize how much you talked about her message with others. In fact, you might have whole friendships built on talking about what the Monger thinks. Friendships where all you did was get together and bash other people or talk about how awful you look, etc. Friendships based on your Monger. That realization is *hard* and painful. I get it.

Life isn't black and white. While our Monger doesn't serve us and drama and distraction don't serve us, we might still miss it because even though it was painful it could be fun. But over time we find that release elsewhere. We make new friends and find healthy ways to take care of ourselves and be understanding of ourselves. We start building a life based on our values and have less need for the drama and distraction that our Monger provided. But remember, anytime we change lifelong habits or behaviors it takes a period of an adjustment.

And yes, life is so much better without the Monger being in charge. It is so satisfying to hear the kind, trusted voice of our Biggest Fan instead of the mean, shaming Monger voice.

Acknowledgments

There are so many people who have made this book possible. First, I want to thank all the clients I have worked with individually and in groups. Without your stories, feedback, and questions, I would not have pushed so hard to find a solution to quieting the Monger voice. I am blessed each day to work with such courageous, strong individuals who are trying to live a happier, more fulfilling life.

My editor, Amy Scott. You took my rough draft and made it readable. Thank you. Thanks to the team at Amelia Studios for bringing my characters to life, you exceeded my expectations.

My husband. Words cannot express your support. The late nights working, the endless discussions of Mongers and Biggest Fans, and the consistent feedback are just a few of your amazing aspects. You are a gift to my life that I am consistently grateful for and I don't know what I would do without you.

My mom. You introduced me to the world of self-help. Leo Buscaglia, John Bradshaw, Marianne Williamson, and Wayne Dyer were a regular part of our conversations growing up. Thank you for giving me the gifts of roots and wings.

My dad. You taught me the power of integrity, perseverance, and showing up. You are the inspiration for this book. I only wish you were here to read it. I miss you every day.

Notes

CHAPTER 1 MEET YOUR MONGER

[1] "Monger," Definition 2, *Merriam-Webster.com*, accessed August 26, 2017, http://www.merriam-webster.com/dictionary/monger.

CHAPTER 2 MYTHS THAT KEEP US STRESSED

[1] Julie Peterman, "Because Sometimes 'Doing the Work' Takes Work: Reclaiming My Self Care Beyond Baths & Wine," *The Body Is Not An Apology*, accessed August 3, 2017, http://thebodyisnotanapology.com/magazine/disabilities-wait-see-submission/

[2] Morissette, A.," Incomplete." *Flavors of Entanglement,* Universal Music Publishing Group, 2008.

[3] Tara Brach, Radical Acceptance: Embracing Your Life with the Heart of a Buddha (New York: Bantam Books, 2004), 3.

[4] Mai-Ly N. Steers et al., "Seeing Everyone Else's Highlight Reels: How Facebook Usage Is Linked to Depressive Symptoms," *Journal of Social and Clinical Psychology*, 33, no. 8 (2014): 701–731, https://doi.org/10.1521/jscp.2014.33.8.701.

[5] Agnes De Mille, Martha: The Life and Work of Martha Graham (New York: Random House, 1991).

CHAPTER 3 WHAT DOESN'T WORK AND WHY

[1] University of Hertfordshire, "Self-Acceptance Could Be the Key to a Happier Life, Yet It's the Happy Habit Many People Practice the Least," ScienceDaily, March 7, 2014, www.sciencedaily.com/releases /2014/03/140307111016.htm.

[2] Joanne V. Wood et al., "Positive Self-Statements: Power for Some, Peril for Others," *Psychological Science* 20, no. 7 (2009): 860–866, https://doi.org/10.1111/j.1467-9280.2009.02370.x.

[3] Gabriele Oettingen, "Don't Think Too Positive," *Aeon*, July 25, 2016, http://aeon.co/essays/thinking-positive-is-a-surprisingly-risky-manoeuvre.

[4] Oliver Burkeman, "The Power of Negative Thinking," *New York Times*, August 4, 2012, http://www.nytimes.com/2012/08/05/opinion/sunday/the-positive-power-of-negative-thinking.html.

CHAPTER 6 A.S.K. STEP 1: ACKNOWLEDGE WHAT YOU ARE FEELING

[1] Ruth Whippman, America the Anxious: How Our Pursuit of Happiness Is Creating a Nation of Nervous Wrecks (New York: St. Martin's Press, 2016), 92.

[2] *Inside Out*, directed by Pete Docter (Emeryville, CA: Pixar Animation Studios, 2015).

[3] Eric L. Garland et al., "Thought Suppression, Impaired Regulation of Urges, and Addiction-Stroop Predict Affect-Modulated Cue-Reactivity among Alcohol Dependent Adults," *Biological Psychology* 89, no. 1 (2012): 87–93, https://doi.org/10.1016/ j.biopsycho. 2011. 09.010.

[4] Susan David, Emotional Agility: Get Unstuck, Embrace Change, and Thrive in Work and Life (New York: Random House, 2016), 45.

[5] Jill Bolte Taylor, My Stroke of Insight: A Brain Scientist's Personal Journey (New York: Penguin Books, 2006), 146.

[6] Matthew D. Lieberman et al., "Putting Feelings into Words: Affect Labeling Disrupts Amygdala Activity to Affective Stimuli," *Psychol. Sci.* 18, no. 5 (May 1, 2007): 421–428, https://doi.org/10.1111/j.1467-9280.2007.01916.x.

[7] Lisa J. Burklund et al., "The Common and Distinct Neural Bases of Affect Labeling and Reappraisal in Healthy Adults," *Frontiers in Psychology* 5, (March 24, 2014), https://doi.org/10.3389/fpsyg.2014.00221.

CHAPTER 7 A.S.K. STEP 2: SLOW DOWN AND GET INTO YOUR BODY

[1] Vicki Brower, "Mind–Body Research Moves towards the Mainstream: Mounting Evidence for the Role of the Mind in Disease and Healing Is Leading to a Greater Acceptance of Mind–Body Medicine," *EMBO Reports,* EMBO Press, April 1, 2006, https://doi.org/10.1038/sj.embor.7400671.

[2] Amy Cuddy, *Presence: Bringing Your Boldest Self to Your Biggest Challenges* (New York: Little, Brown and Company, 2015), 269.

CHAPTER 9 WHAT'S MOST IMPORTANT TO YOU?

[1] Brené Brown, "Exercise: How Values Light the Way," Brené Brown, LLC, 2015, http://cdn.courageworks.com/files/0782c7e3cd35c24461ec9ed10e580ec247cae806_original.pdf?1452372876.

[2] "Value," Definition 4, *Merriam-Webster.com*, accessed August 26, 2017, http://www.merriam-webster.com/dictionary/value.

CHAPTER 10 CHANGE IS POSSIBLE—IT JUST ISN'T EASY

[1] Carl Rogers, *On Becoming a Person: A Therapist's View of Psychotherapy* (Boston: Houghton Mifflin Company, 1961).

[2] *What about Bob?* directed by Frank Oz (Los Angeles: Buena Vista Pictures Distribution, Inc., 1991).

Index

172 | INDEX

About the Author

Nancy Jane Smith, MSEd, is a Licensed Professional Counselor and trainer. She is owner of Live Happier. An expert on stress and anxiety she has a passion for helping people quiet their inner Monger so they can live happier and successful lives based on their terms. Nancy has a private practice where she works individually with clients and also speaks to corporations and organizations helping people build more productive less stressed lives

She lives in Columbus, Ohio with her husband and their furry children.

To receive more information on Nancy Jane Smith, visit www.live-happier.com